# NEW HAMPSHIRE

# BEER

# NEW HAMPSHIRE

# BEER

## BREWING FROM SEA TO SUMMIT

### BRIAN ALDRICH & MICHAEL MEREDITH

FOREWORD BY TOD MOTT

AMERICAN PALATE

Published by American Palate
A Division of The History Press
Charleston, SC 29403
www.historypress.net

Copyright © 2014 by Brian Aldrich and Michael Meredith
All rights reserved

Parts of this book have appeared, in a different form, on the Seacoast Beverage
Lab Podcast at SBLPodcast.com.

First published 2014

Manufactured in the United States

ISBN 978.1.62619.425.0

Library of Congress CIP data applied for.

## BRIAN

*To my dad for introducing me to the world of beer and home-brewing. To my mom, one of my biggest fans, who made me the kindhearted person I am. To my lovely wife and forever bar mate, Lisa, for going on brewery trips and always putting a smile on my face during the process of writing this book.*

## MIKE

*To my loving family and friends who have supported me my entire life. To my parents, who always taught me to work hard and good things will happen. To Brian Aldrich for giving me my first book on craft beer, introducing me to the craft beer scene and always being there to cheers a brew or two.*

# CONTENTS

# CONTENTS

# FOREWORD

The year was 2003, and I answered David Yarrington's (executive brewer at Smuttynose Brewing Company) inquiry about knowing any brewers looking for work by stating, "I'll look into it." The more I thought about his question, the more I thought, "Yeah, I know somebody looking for brewing work… ME!" At the time, I was the brewer at the Tap in Haverhill, Massachusetts. I had been working there for about six months when Dave called. In those days, I was a bit frustrated because my previous employment opportunity was a bust, the clientele at the Tap was not quite established as of yet and my beer was languishing in the serving tanks a little too long for my liking. So I called Dave back and asked if I could interview for the Portsmouth Brewery job. He was a bit taken aback, but he said yes. I went to Portsmouth and interviewed with Peter Egelston, owner of Portsmouth Brewery (P-Brew) and Smuttynose Brewing Company, and David for four hours in what is affectionately called the fish bowl, due to the surrounding glass façade. I landed the job and so began my introduction with beers brewed in the Granite State—New Hampshire, or, as some of the brewing cognoscenti refer to it, "the Shire." There were only a handful of breweries at that time, and Peter had been instrumental in the passage of the brewpub laws, allowing for the rise of those ever-so-humble establishments. P-Brew has been cranking out beer for over twenty years, of which I was at the helm for eight and a half.

The most exciting event that happened during my tenure at P-Brew was the BeerAdvocate's publishing its "best of" list in 2008 and having one of my beers on the list. What started as simply a great beer received world-class recognition and turned into the year's "must-have beer." That changed everything at P-Brew, and as some say, the rest is history.

In any event, when I took the job at Portsmouth Brewery, there were only a handful of microbreweries and brewpubs in New Hampshire. I knew most of the players and most of the beer involved. The beer was good beer, and there were some outstanding brewers in New Hampshire. Now, eleven years later, the beer scene has totally transformed to a superhighway of craft beer. In the past three years, we have seen an explosion of craft beer all across the United States, and the trend is not getting any slower or smaller. What I get a charge out of is how passionate all the old guard and the new players are about their trade/craft/art. I have told the story many times, but beer is the combination of art and science. The majority of U.S. beer drinkers are blinded by the yellow fizzy mass-produced light lagers synonymous with the big three American breweries. The large brewing companies produce beer on a scale of volume economics. Bigger, more efficient equipment using less-than-high-quality ingredients creates a less expensive product. The economy of large-scale brewing allows for money to go toward marketing rather than the higher-priced, better-quality ingredients. Where the big guys falter is in the diversity of beer styles. This is what craft is all about: the decision to use great ingredients and produce a variety of styles. Today's brewers are not concerned with the parameters of the how but more of the what. The resurgence of craft brewing, the farm-to-table and slow-food movements plus sustainability and transparency have become the way of becoming a viable entity in one's community. It is the community we are reaching out to, not the world. Think globally; act locally. New Hampshire's local communities respect the movement, and the brewers respect their communities. So folks from "the Shire," keep drinking the great beer brewed in your state, and the brewers will continue to impress you with the integrity of the beers they produce.

Cheers!
**TOD MOTT**
*Spring 2014*

# INTRODUCTION

Frank Jones. A name synonymous with beer and New Hampshire. There was a time when the Frank Jones Brewery of Portsmouth, New Hampshire, was the largest brewery in America. At the brewery's peak, 250,000 barrels of beer were rolling out of the brewery on Islington Street. Now the brewery is gone, but the building remains, as does the legacy it holds.

New Hampshire is the state I have called home since late 2008. Admittedly, I wasn't much of a beer drinker at the time. Looking back, I realize I was in the calm before the storm of another craft beer revolution. Sitting in the Portsmouth Brewery for the first time in August 2008, I was captivated by the joy on people's faces as they drank beer that was made in the same building. Looking through the glass into the brew house and seeing Tod Mott making the beers that would inspire me to start writing about beer is an experience I will never forget.

In 2010, I began to write about the craft beer scene in the seacoast area of New Hampshire. Since then, the amount of breweries in the state has more than doubled. When approached to write this book, I knew I couldn't do it alone. I wanted to share this adventure. I believe craft beer should be enjoyed with friends and family, so I set off on this craft beer trek with my longtime friend Mike Meredith.

New Hampshire has a deep, rich history when it comes to beer. The breweries of the 1990s have paved the way for the up-and-coming breweries of today. We wanted to understand what the beer scene was like for the

Seacoast jetty located in Odiorne Point State Park in Rye, New Hampshire. *Photo courtesy of Corey O'Connor, www.coreyoconnorphoto.com.*

breweries that have been operating for decades and how their trials and tribulations have helped the breweries of the 2000s. A glass will be raised to the past, but as the craft beer scene continues to grow, it is important to highlight the present as we look toward the future.

We hope this book inspires you to get out and make your own craft beer adventure. We traveled the state to each and every brewery in this book to meet the brewers, drink the beer and document facts you may not have known about the history of your favorite brewery. We also put in some of our experiences from our travels. What is great about the beer industry is that the brewers do not hide in the shadows. You will see the brewers out and about town, enjoying a beer—be it their own beer or someone else's—and pouring beers at festivals with a smile. Sitting down and talking to everyone, over a beer of course, is what rounded out this experience. Each brewery tells a unique story through its beer and its history as a brewery.

Let us not forget the places to drink the beers. While many breweries have tasting rooms and growler fills or pubs, there are plenty of great bars where you will find these great beers on tap. When traveling, it is important to find a bar where you can get the beer on tap. New Hampshire has no shortage in watering holes and, much like the breweries, offer their own spin on the concept of a bar. From craft beer–centric to dive bars, they are as important to the state as the breweries.

By the time you read this book, there will surely be an increased number of breweries in New Hampshire. This is an example of the growing craft beer scene, and we are excited to see what the future holds. Cheers!

**BRIAN ALDRICH**

1

# FRANK JONES BREWERY

In 1858, Frank Jones began working at John Swindell's Brewery in Portsmouth. A few short years later, he bought out the shares and renamed it Frank Jones Brewery. In 1865, a local newspaper ran this story on Jones, describing the brewing process and future plans of growth:

*In connection with this brewery, Mr. Jones has, within a year or two, erected a large building for a malt house, and here the process of brewing (malting) commences. In the bins, lay [sic] immense piles of pure Canada barley, 25,000 to 33,000 bushels, certainly, good looking enough to eat as ale does to drink after the batch is made. About 500 bushels of grain is [sic] thrown into the great circular wooden water tank, the sides of which are higher than your head, located in the lower room, and soaked for a couple of days. Then, having been winnowed of all bad kernels, peas, other grains, weed seeds, etc., by dipping off these extraneous matters, which all float on the top of the water, and which are sold at a price for light food for horses, and for pigs, hens and etc...the soaked and perfect barley are [sic] spread on the smooth, clean floor to the depth of six inches or so, and there lies for a few days to swell and sprout, heat and ferment. There are three of these piles or beds of barley, of 500 bushels each, spread over the floor, in different stages of preparation.*

*From here the grain goes into the drying room, the floor of which is iron, punctured with innumerable little holes, like a strainer or sieve, and the coal fires in the furnaces which are never allowed to go out, day or night, the year round. When entirely dry, the grain, which is now malt, or malted barley, is conveyed to the brewery proper, and cracked in a mill, then soaked again, this time in hot water, pure from the Portsmouth Aqueduct, and placed on another sieve or strainer, and the liquid caught below, which, as extract of barley, is all of the grain which is wanted. The residue is the "Brewers Grain" which is sold for food for animals, and is a valuable manure.*

*Hops are now added to this liquid extract in such quantities as to produce ale of desired strength and quality, whether stock, amber or cream; and, after fermenting to the proper point, is barreled for use. In pure ale there is no other ingredient besides these, water and hops. But adulteration by means of "quassis" (the wooden bark of tropical trees) instead of hops, may be made at greatly reduced prices…We understand that Mr. Jones' accommodations, spacious and complete as they are, are by no means sufficient for his increasing business; and he has extensive stables and sheds already in the course of erection, and contemplates considerable additions to his brewery and malt house.*

Frank Jones was a jack of all trades, owning businesses from hotels and restaurants to utilities companies and banks. Jones also was elected mayor of Portsmouth twice during the time he was operating the brewery. In the years leading up to Prohibition, Jones made extensive additions to his brewery, adding a barrel house, malt house, bottling line and clock tower. At its peak, the Frank Jones Brewery was producing 250,000 barrels of beer a year, the most of any brewery in the United States. After Prohibition, Jones sold the equipment from the brewery, but the brand continued to be circulated by the Eldridge Brewing Company of Portsmouth, Jones's old competition. Eldridge produced the beer at the old Frank Jones Brewery for a number of years, stopping in 1950 when the brewery closed. If you take a walk through Portsmouth, you will see a number of buildings and businesses that Frank Jones had a hand in creating. The largest of Jones's contributions is, of course, the brewery, the building of which remains standing on Islington Street.

# 2
# ANHEUSER-BUSCH

## 221 DANIEL WEBSTER HIGHWAY, MERRIMACK
## (603) 595-1202 | WWW.ANHEUSER-BUSCH.COM |
## FOUNDED 1970

The Anheuser-Busch Brewery is the oldest brewery still active in the state of New Hampshire. This facility, located at 221 Daniel Webster Highway in historic Merrimack, New Hampshire, was established in 1970. This facility has been going strong in the Granite State for over forty years and services the New England landscape, including Maine, Vermont, New Hampshire, Massachusetts, Connecticut and Rhode Island. Just think, there are over fourteen million people that reside in the New England region, and this one facility is designated to service all of them. Most craft breweries distribute on a small scale in a few states. Being a part of the largest brewing organization on the planet allows Anheuser-Busch Brewery the benefit of reaching more consumers on a daily basis. It has helped it establish its name as a staple in the beer world for decades and has made it a household name.

Their facility is nestled on a sprawling 294 acres of land filled with hop gardens, stone paths and, of course, horse stables that house a team of legendary Budweiser Clydesdales. Spanning over 865,000 square feet, this location produces eight beers in the AB lineup. These beers include Budweiser, Bud Light, Natural Light, Busch, Busch Light, Michelob Light, Michelob ULTRA and Redbridge. They have redefined what it means to produce beer in terms of quality and sheer quantity. Pumping out approximately one hundred trucks per day (that's a lot of beer), this brewery has become a cornerstone in the brewing landscape in New Hampshire.

The Anheuser-Busch Brewing company was founded in 1852 in St. Louis, Missouri. Over the years, it has grown to be one of the largest brewers of

*Above*: Anheuser-Busch facility in Merrimack, New Hampshire. *Photo courtesy of Scott Louis Photography, http:// swlouis.com.*

*Left*: Anheuser-Busch Hop Garden on display at the Merrimack, New Hampshire location. *Photo courtesy of Scott Louis Photography, http:// swlouis.com.*

A pint being poured for the patrons touring the Anheuser-Busch facility in Merrimack, New Hampshire. *Photo courtesy of Scott Louis Photography, http://swlouis.com.*

beer in history. Owning and operating thirteen large capacity breweries in the United States, the brewery is, as of 2008, under the AB InBev company, which is the largest producer of beer in the world. The company as a whole employs over 150,000 people in twenty-four countries around the globe. The Anheuser-Busch Brewery has worked to establish its home-grown roots. Although the brewery is a part of a large international body, it hires, trains and develops people in its plants' local communities. Many amazing brewers work at the Merrimack, New Hampshire facility, and these people work to create brews for the people of New Hampshire and the entire New England region.

The tour at the brewery is an outstanding education in brewing on a large scale. We recommend you carve out an afternoon to see what brewing on the macro level is all about. Overall, the brewing experience at any brewery—whether it be a small one-barrel system or a large, macro facility like the one located in Merrimack—is a beer lover's dream. The dedication and precision it takes to brew beer of the same quality day in and day out is not an easy task for any operation. The Anheuser-Busch Brewery prides itself on the quality and consistency of its brews each day. Overall, the brewing community in New Hampshire applauds the operations of the

Anheuser-Busch Brewery. The entire community prides itself on quality and consistency, and the brewery has authored the book on it. Personally, any brewery that takes the time to brew consistent beer on a daily, monthly and yearly basis gets a thumbs up in our eyes.

# THE TOUR

Nestled in the scenic New England countryside, the Anheuser-Busch Brewery in Merrimack, New Hampshire, offers complimentary tours throughout the year that allow guests to see how some of the world's best beers are brewed by talented brew masters. In addition to the history of Anheuser-Busch and the Merrimack brewery, the tour includes information about the company's extraordinary local and national initiatives to help protect and preserve the environment. Visitors can also get up close with the world-famous Budweiser Clydesdales at the Merrimack Clydesdale Hamlet. The gentle giants have appeared in wildly popular television commercials over the years and represent a special part of Anheuser-Busch's history. At the conclusion of the tour, free samples of freshly brewed Anheuser-Busch beers are offered to guests twenty-one years and older.

Anheuser-Busch Tour Center interior in Merrimack, New Hampshire. *Photo courtesy of Scott Louis Photography, http://swlouis.com.*

# 3
# PORTSMOUTH BREWERY

## 56 MARKET STREET, PORTSMOUTH
## (603) 431-1115 | WWW.PORTSMOUTHBREWERY.COM |
## FOUNDED 1991

There are two smells that best describe Portsmouth—the smell of roasting coffee from Breaking New Grounds on Market Square and the smell of beer being brewed at Portsmouth Brewery. There is no escaping that giant golden mug of beer that hangs outside on Market Street. Peter Egelston is the man responsible for opening New Hampshire's first brewpub following Prohibition. Peter opened the Northampton Brewery in Massachusetts with his sister, Janet, in 1987 before leaving that brewpub to her and heading to the Granite State. Following the country's craft beer revolution started by Anchor Steam's Fritz Maytag, New Albion's Jack McAuliffe and Sierra Nevada's Ken Grossman, Peter and Janet Egelston were at the forefront of the New England craft beer revival.

There wasn't much of a beer scene in New England in 1987. In 1986, Karen and David Geary opened the D.L. Geary Brewing Company, and Steve Mason opened Catamount Brewing Company in Windsor, Vermont. Dan Kenary and Rich Doyle opened the Harpoon Brewery in the summer of 1987 in Boston, Massachusetts, and Sam Adams's Boston Lager was beginning to make the rounds at bars. Because the concept of a brewpub was new in New England, Peter and Janet Egelston were making the rules as they went along. "No one knew what we were doing. Beer at that time was still beer with a lowercase *b*, all the same," Peter says.

The Egelstons opened the doors at Northampton Brewery in 1987 with Amber Lager and Golden Lager. "In those days, people just wanted a beer

Portsmouth Brewery logo. *Photo courtesy of Portsmouth Brewery.*

and didn't understand the concept that beer could be made in the same place you eat and drink," Peter explains. The difference between then and now is that first beer. An introduction to beer for you today may not necessarily be the same as others from the '80s. There were no local double IPAs or imperial stouts.

Peter and Janet's first task was justifying their existence. People wanted to know why they were making beer in a small building when the bigger breweries were making beer in bigger facilities in the middle of the country. Because the concept was new, they could afford to make a lot of mistakes and get away with them, both with beer and food. "People's standards were lower back then because the concept of a brewpub was so new. Nowadays, making really good beer today just gets you a seat at the table," Peter says. He combed through resources such as Charlie Papazian's book *The Complete Joy of Homebrewing* and David Line's *Brewing Beers Like Those You Buy* to gain ideas for his own formulas.

After operating Northampton Brewery for years, Peter wanted a second location. He began scouting in an unfriendly legal climate. After searching for locations in many New England states, Egelston ended up in Portsmouth, New Hampshire. Peter had called the liquor commissioner and got an encouraging response. "We were wondering when someone was going to come open a brewpub here," Peter recalls the commissioner saying. "They were very welcoming." At the time, Market Street in Portsmouth wasn't considered the prime real estate it is today. The center of the tourist attractions was one street over on State Street. Peter left the Northampton Brewery to Janet, and after holding the position from 1987 to 1991, Peter had to give up the reigns as brewer. The job went to his former assistant brewer, Rick Quackenbush, who held the position for years. The first brewer at the Portsmouth Brewery was Paul Murphy.

"We would have built the brewery very differently if we had twenty years of hindsight. You will find brewpubs of a certain age are built around seven barrels as a standard due to the abundance of grundy tanks—or British cellar tanks, which hold seven barrels of beer." Around the early to mid-'90s, many small British breweries were going out of business. There was value in selling their equipment to new breweries that were starting up in the United States. When you walk into the brewery today, you will have an array of seating options. From the "fishbowl" in the front of the brewery that has a window looking out on busy Market Street, the side restaurant, main area, bar area, upper area and downstairs lounge. "The feeling of Portsmouth Brewery is a series of little neighborhoods," Pete says. The upper area of the pub was a "happy accident to solve an architectural problem." The fourteen-barrel fermenters were too tall to fit in the space to begin with, so Peter had to raise the roof. Now you can look down on the brewers as you eat lunch. Those "neighborhoods" make the three-hundred-seat brewpub much more intimate.

Getting off the ground, Peter and brewer Paul took the path of least resistance and cloned beers that were successful at Northampton Brewery. Portsmouth Pale Ale was Northampton Pale Ale with a different name. This beer lives on today through the beer sold exclusively to Common Man restaurants. It was a real simple beer with two different kinds of malts and two different kinds of hops. Other beers included the Weizenheimer and the Black Cat Stout. Those beers can still be found at both Northampton and Portsmouth breweries at various times throughout the year.

While Peter wanted to start with beers he knew were safe, it was important to him that the brewers at the Portsmouth site develop their own identity. Brewing beers in house did not stop the bigger U.S. breweries from knocking on their door. In the spring of 1991, Portsmouth Brewery was approached by a macrobrewery and asked when the brewpub would be ready to put the larger brewery's beer on tap. Peter explained that Portsmouth Brewery planned on selling only the beers it made in house. "You guys are never going to stay in business if you don't sell our beer," Peter was told. For Portsmouth Brewery, not selling macro beers had nothing to do with the bigger breweries. "We have always felt like everyone who walks into the Portsmouth Brewery and orders someone else's beer is an opportunity to win them over with our beer. There are a lot of people out there who love good beer; they just don't know it yet."

Paul Murphy was head brewer at Portsmouth Brewery until Smuttynose opened, when he transitioned there. Sean Navish took over for Paul, and in 2003, Tod Mott took the helm. Mott came from Haverhill, Massachusetts, where he was brewing at the Tap Brew Pub. "We signed Tod Mott at the same time the Red Sox signed Curt Schilling, and they went on to win the World Series, and we felt we did the same," Peter said. Mott's Bottle Rocket IPA knocked Portsmouth Pale Ale out of rotation due to its popularity. What he may be most known for is his port wood–aged Russian imperial stout known as Kate the Great. The beer had minimal fanfare until 2007, when all of a sudden, *Beer Advocate* magazine named it the best beer in America. Peter saw it and said, "That's interesting." After seeing this, Peter asked Tod to pick a random date and time that he would put Kate on tap again. Peter put a simple countdown clock on the brewpub's website pointing to the date and time of the Kate the Great release four months away. "That's what started the anticipation," Peter said. The date came, and there was a line down Market Street. In the second year, they began to hand out calendar pages as a way to organize bottle sales. Thirsty beer fans would line up to get a page, and when their month was called, they could enter the brewery to have the beer from the taps and buy a bottle. For the final two years of Kate the Great Day, the Portsmouth Brewery teamed up with local charities to release scratch tickets a week in advance for a chance to purchase bottles of Kate the Great, raising thousands of dollars. The final Kate the Great Day was on March 5, 2012. The day started at 2:45 a.m., when two friends got in line, and ended at 6:45 p.m., when the final drops of the beer poured from the taps. The entirety of the final day was captured on webcam to give those across the world the glimpse at one of the biggest beer release days in the world.

In July 2012, Tod Mott resigned from the Portsmouth Brewery, passing the torch to his assistant brewer Tyler Jones. While Mott's legacy at the brewery will forever be embedded in the memories of beer fans across the world, he hasn't hung up his brewing supplies just yet. Tod will be opening a brewery in southern Maine, where he can continue brewing great beer. Even though Kate the Great may seem like Tod Mott's biggest contribution to the Portsmouth Brewery, he made a number of beers that were essential in the craft beer uprising of the seacoast. Mott also brought a lot of big names to Portsmouth, such as Mitch Steele of Stone Brewing Company and Sam Calagione of Dogfish Head. Shortly before leaving, Mott also brewed a beer with an all-star list of brewers for the Portsmouth Brewery's twentieth anniversary. Twenty brewers added twenty different malts and twenty different hops to the beer.

The roster included:

1) Tod Mott, Alumni Portsmouth Brewery
2) Tyler Jones, Portsmouth Brewery

3) Tyson Demurs, Smuttynose Brewing Company
4) Peter Egelston, alumnus Portsmouth Brewery/Smuttynose/Northampton Brewery
5) Chuck Doughty, alumnus Portsmouth Brewery/Smuttynose
6) Paul Murphy, alumnus Portsmouth Brewery/Smuttynose
7) Sean Navish, alumnus Portsmouth Brewery
8) Keith Gosselin, alumnus Portsmouth Brewery/Smuttynose
9) J.T. Thompson, alumnus Portsmouth Brewery/Smuttynose
10) Charlie Ireland, Smuttynose
11) Chris Kluun, Smuttynose
12) Tom Ostromecky, Smuttynose
13) Zach Boda, alumnus Portsmouth Brewery/current Allagash
14) Jason Perkins, Allagash
15) Andy Schwartz, Craft Brewers Alliance
16) Jim Sipp, Craft Brewers Alliance
17) Alex Kopf, Craft Brewers Alliance
18) Will Meyers, Cambridge Brewing Company

Portsmouth Brewery pint and menu in the Jimmy LaPanza Lounge. *Photo courtesy of Michael Meredith.*

19) Greg Oullette, Martha's Exchange
20) Steve Schmidt, alumnus Meantime Brewing Company
21) Yvan de Baets, Brasserie de la Senne
22) Paul Davis, Prodigal Brewing Company

The Portsmouth Brewery remains today as one of the highlights on the seacoast for both food and beer. Continued efforts to donate to charity live on in the form of wooden tokens on certain days for every beer sold. The Jimmy LaPanza Lounge is a great place to hang out with friends and play pool, shuffleboard or hold private events. The newly revamped tap list now holds a combination of sixteen beers from Portsmouth Brewery, Smuttynose Brewing Company and other breweries around the country, as well as a couple cask lines for those in love with Real Ale.

# Brewer Spotlight

## Tyler Jones

Tyler was studying chemical engineering at the University of New Hampshire when he found a home-brew kit in his closet. "This was the first blend of art and science I had ever found," Tyler said. After catching the brewing bug, he got his Master Brewer Certificate from UC–Davis in 2006. His first job in the industry was at Mercury Brewing Company in Ipswich, Massachusetts. There he learned to brew from the bottom up: cleaning tanks, driving forklifts and working on recipes of varying sizes. In 2007, he applied for a position at the Portsmouth Brewery and began working under Tod Mott. The team of Tod and Tyler was a great era for both locals and tourists to witness. They both thrived off customer interaction. You could watch them make the beer from inside the restaurant and then see them walking around the restaurant, beer in hand, saying hello to everyone. For his first beer, Tyler created a barleywine. "Start big or go home," Tyler said. Jones went on to introduce the Gose, a salty/sour style of beer. One of his claims to fame was a beer he brewed for his wedding, the Ginga Ninja, an IPA brewed with ginger. Tyler was the assistant until 2012, when he left to work at Smuttynose Brewing Company for a few months. When Tod Mott stepped down at the Portsmouth Brewery, Tyler came back as head brewer.

Tyler brews what *he* wants, which is certainly contradictory to many other breweries in the country that brew for the consumer. Turns out, though, that the beers he wants to brew are the beers people love to drink. The beauty of being in a big tourism area of New Hampshire is the beers that are on this week may not be the same as next week. This customer flow gives Tyler the opportunity to try many different styles of beer. You will certainly find something you like, and Tyler will help you find it. If he isn't available, there is bound to be a local or two who can help you decide. His assistants Tyler Sildve and Matt Gallagher experiment a lot with cask beers. From a milk stout with chocolate chip cookies to a cream ale with basil, there is always something for the adventurous at the Portsmouth Brewery.

# 4

# MARTHA'S EXCHANGE RESTAURANT & BREWERY

## 185 MAIN STREET, NASHUA
## (603) 883-8781 | WWW.MARTHAS-EXCHANGE.COM |
## FOUNDED 1993

People usually think of Nashua due to the Daniel Webster highway, where many go for shops and malls selling any product under the sun. Because of Nashua's location, many residents of Massachusetts drive mere minutes for tax-free shopping. Ten minutes north of this shopping mecca, you will find Main Street in Nashua. This street is like a scene out of yesteryear: a street packed with shops, bars and businesses and, nestled in the middle of it all, Martha's Exchange Restaurant & Brewery.

Martha's Exchange welcomed us into what appears, at first glance, to be a true foodie's paradise. This dining and brewing location wasn't always known for its good food and libations. Originally, this brewery/restaurant located right in the heart of downtown Nashua was known for another guilty pleasure—candy. Serving up a wide variety of sweets from chocolate turtles to sour gummies, this candy shop still catches the attention of the everyday restaurant-goer and the passersby on the street just like it did when it first started back in 1932.

Over eighty years ago, the great-aunt of Bill and Chris Fokas immigrated to the United States, where she started a small confection shop known as Martha's Sweet Shoppe. Speculation on the name's origin comes from a popular candy in that time period known as "Martha Washington Candy." In 1944, Bill and Chris's father, James Fokas, took over the business after returning from the war. Over time, the sweet shop expanded its menu to create an eatery, and Martha's Sweet Shoppe and Luncheonette was born.

The sweet shop and luncheonette was a local landmark for almost fifty years, but in 1985, James Fokas's sons, Bill and Chris, took the reins of the family business and gave it a massive overhaul. A two-year renovation of the existing space gave birth to what is now known as Martha's Exchange. Five short years later, the brothers decided to capitalize on a new trend in the States—hand-crafted beers.

In 1993, Martha's Exchange added to its operations Nashua's first and only microbrewery, and it is still thriving to this day.

Priding itself on its craft beers, Martha's Exchange doesn't hide its seven-barrel system in a separate room off the restaurant. It is right out in the open for all to see. It is truly amazing that this system fits in the small space that is allocated for it. The gorgeous copper system outlines the far wall for all to gaze on as they drink, dine and relax with their friends and family. After taking in the scenery over lunch, we had the privilege of walking the brewery with head brewer Greg Ouellette.

Celebrating its twentieth anniversary of brewing in 2014, Martha's Exchange is the second-oldest brewery in the state behind Portsmouth Brewery. Greg started with Martha's Exchange in 2001 and will be celebrating twelve years of brewing this year. He started his career at IncrediBREW, which is also located in Nashua, for about five years. IncrediBREW is a brewery and winery where customers go to create beer and wine on site. It's a unique experience that allows people in the community to try their hand at home-brewing beer, wine or even soda.

Gaining a tremendous amount of experience early on, Greg was anxious to dive into the brewing industry. After years of trying, a fellow colleague suggested that he take a look at Martha's Exchange right down the road.

Greg was excited to take on the new role as head brewer and was thrown into it very quickly. His first brew was a full-bodied amber ale that he was quite proud of. The owners were looking for true variety in the brews. Ranging from light-bodied ales to dark, robust porters, Greg hit the ground running and went full steam ahead.

Martha's Exchange is unique in today's craft beer world in the sense that it offers both macro beers and spirits at its restaurant. Patrons truly have a wide variety to choose from on any given day. Diversification is the name of the game at this hopping downtown brewery. The place wants you to have what you want. However, when discussing the beer list with the staff, Greg always wants everyone to know that Martha's Exchange is a brewery first. Having the community try its beer is important. Allowing people to sample and try beers they might not normally go for is a great stepping stone into the craft brew world. When discussing this with Greg, he referred to these easy-to-drink, light craft beers as "gateway beers." Over time, many people in the Nashua community have steered away from their traditional macro beers to try one of the beers at Martha's. There's truly something for everyone who enjoys hand-crafted beer. Once people try one of these delicious brews, they rarely go back.

Martha's Exchange offers a unique experience for its patrons. They can witness Greg brewing firsthand. The site's open-air system allows people to look on as he brews. Greg joked with us, saying, "Most days I am just cleaning the tanks or mopping the floors, but a typical brew day can last up to eight hours. I have nowhere to hide!" It truly is a sight to see. The brushed copper tanks are a rare thing to find in today's brewing scene. Modern tanks are silver with a brushed steel look. The copper-covered style is a look into the past that truly speaks to Martha's Exchange and the atmosphere it portrays.

As we finished up our tour with Greg, he brought us down below to view the grundy tanks. *Grundy* is a term adopted by the North American craft brewing industry for cellar tanks built in the United Kingdom in the early 1950s. The inexpensive, mass-produced tanks have been utilized in almost every stage of the brewing process. These tanks don't pop up very often, and we were lucky enough to view them with Greg.

After an informative and personal tour with Greg, we sat down at the bar to enjoy his pride and joy, the Abbot's Habit Belgian Tripel. This beer is a Belgian pale ale with a staggering 9 percent ABV (alcohol by volume). The higher alcohol content is masked by a smooth delicious flavor that is good to the last drop. He only tackles the tripel style once a year and looks forward to the challenge of wrangling this Belgian delight. We toasted to twenty more years and headed on our way.

Martha's Exchange offers a wide variety of macrobrews and spirits alongside its hand-crafted beers. The atmosphere of this establishment is hybrid in nature. With a vintage feel, this horseshoe-shaped marble-topped bar allows people to enjoy a pint while reading or engaging in the latest sporting event on the brewpub's many TVs. This downtown hot spot caters to a wide variety of individuals. Ranging from the daytime lunch crowd to the youthful party scene at night, this establishment carries on with full force and gusto. When the sun goes down on Main Street in Nashua, the party kicks off at Martha's Exchange.

# 5
# MILLY'S TAVERN

## 500 NORTH COMMERCIAL STREET, MANCHESTER
## (603) 625-4444 | WWW.MILLYSTAVERN.COM |
## FOUNDED 1994

One of the most unique breweries in New Hampshire is one of the oldest. Milly's Tavern is both a brewpub and more recently a brewery that distributes beer all over New Hampshire. The brewery is the brainchild of head brewer Peter Telge. Unlike many brewers, Peter didn't have a home-brewing background. He started as a restaurant and bar manager in the mid-1980s. He was, however, a lover of beer. In 1992, he went to the Boston Beer Festival. He was blown away by how great the beers were and how cool the brewers were and thought Manchester could use a brewpub.

"A perfect location to open a brewery would be the Millyard," Peter said. At this point in time, Portsmouth Brewery was just getting going in Portsmouth as well as Martha's Exchange in Nashua. He opened Stark Mill Brewery in 1994. He went to Portland, Maine, to learn how to brew for six weeks. He ordered the equipment and was trained on it by the company who sold it. It was important to him to develop his own recipes due to experiences in the restaurant business where chefs would take their recipes with them when they left. He didn't want brewers to do the same at his brewery. When formulating his beer recipes, Peter created versions of the beers he liked to drink. The John Stark Porter was modeled after Heineken Dark, and Tasha's Red Tail Ale was modeled off Bass Ale. Bass and Heineken were readily available throughout the state. There were very few craft breweries, so tweaking recipes of those beers was the logical place to start. Over the years, he came up with many more recipes, and many of those won medals. Their Milly's Oatmeal Stout won a gold medal at the 1998 World Beer Cup in Rio de Janeiro.

Milly's Tavern growlers and kettles on display in Manchester, New Hampshire. *Photo courtesy of Milly's Tavern.*

In a city run by the bigger macrobreweries, he noticed how hard it was for the start-up breweries to get their beer into bars and beer stores. Now, with more craft breweries in the area, we are starting to see more craft beers on the taps. Peter is on the executive board of the Granite State Brewers Association (see Appendix I for details on GSBA). It is important to him that all brewers support one another by keeping a pulse on legislation and attracting tourists to their breweries, which now more than ever are landmarks in their own right. "We are trying to change a mindset about beer that the state and bar owners have," Peter said. Now that the state is recognizing craft breweries and with the creation of the GSBA, brewing has become a serious topic of discussion in the capital.

Recently, Peter walked into a local bar to announce he was going to start distributing his beers in bottles and on draft throughout the state. The bar owner said the bar would take off another New Hampshire brewery's beer and put his on. Peter didn't like the response. In a state with a growing craft beer scene, we should be seeing bars with as much local craft beer as possible. Bars should not have to substitute one New Hampshire beer for another. He hopes to see every bar in the state have a strong focus on local craft beer. The GSBA will certainly help spread this positive message.

Stark Brewing Company logo. *Photo courtesy of Stark Brewing Company.*

Milly's has an internship program for brewers that is headed by Peter. He trains them on the system from cleaning to brewing and bottling. He tastes beers with them, allows them to try different ingredients and asks, "What flavors are you getting?" or "What could be causing this?" He is imparting twenty years of brewing experience to these interns that will help them develop skills and become great brewers at Milly's. Peter is also curious in his own right, researching new hop strains and styles to unleash on thirsty customers.

Milly's has a 14-barrel brewing system that could output 2,500 barrels a year. Currently it is averaging 500 to 600 barrels a year. To maximize the use of its equipment, Milly's began to distribute beer under the brand Stark Brewing Company in March 2014. This is the same beer you will find at Milly's Tavern, but it is located all over New Hampshire in bars and beer stores. The first beers being distributed are its award-winning Milly's Oatmeal Stout and Mount U Golden Cream Ale. The brewpub's goal is to spread more good beer throughout the state to those who can't come to Manchester to try it firsthand. The pub itself has nineteen beers on tap, all its own making, which you can also purchase in a growler to take home. Pete brews anything from a gluten-free beer, black IPAs, imperial stouts and even a blueberry–pumpkin pie beer. For beers like the pumpkin beer, Peter utilizes the pub's kitchen to hollow out pumpkins that he gets from farmers. Every square inch of the tavern's space is being used efficiently. Peter encourages the cooking staff to try new things with his beers as well as pair dishes with beer.

Milly's is celebrating its twentieth year in 2014. In the twenty years Peter has been at Milly's, he said he is seeing people become more adventurous. As Stark Brewing Company gets off the ground, Peter hopes to use some of his draft lines at Milly's Tavern to showcase other New Hampshire beers—just another perfect example of one of the oldest breweries in New Hampshire supporting other breweries.

# 6
# SMUTTYNOSE BREWING COMPANY

## 105 TOWLE FARM ROAD, HAMPTON
## (603) 436-4026 | WWW.SMUTTYNOSE.COM |
## FOUNDED 1994

Customers at the Portsmouth Brewery were asking Peter Egelston and his sister, Janet, if they had plans distributing their brewpub beers to a wider market. "We didn't really take it that seriously because we had our hands full with the brewpub," Peter said. Shortly after opening Portsmouth Brewery, though, an opportunity arose. The Frank Jones Brewery was holding a bankruptcy auction in late 1993. This was not the Frank Jones Brewery that closed in 1950; this was a different brewery using the Frank Jones name that had a beer made at the now defunct Catamount Brewery in 1991. The brewers at Frank Jones decide to open a location on Heritage Avenue in Portsmouth and soon went bankrupt. Peter attended the auction without the intention to buy; he was more interested in seeing who would acquire the equipment and what they would do with it. The auction ended with bids that were not high enough, so it went private. Later that day, Peter was having lunch with Paul Silva and Jim Beuvais of Ipswich Brewing Company. "They said, 'Why don't we put a number on a piece of paper? It might be fun,'" Peter said. Sure enough, their bid was accepted, and in January 1994, Peter got the keys to the building on Heritage Avenue.

Walking into the 12,500-square-foot building, Peter said to himself, "What did I get myself into?" When Peter opened Portsmouth Brewery, he had a plan of action. But after purchasing the equipment from Frank Jones, he didn't know what to do with it. He didn't have much experience on brewing beer at this scale with little capital. The equipment was used equipment

Smuttynose Brewing Company logo. *Photo courtesy of Smuttynose Brewing Company.*

from Thunder Bay, Ontario, Canada, and over the years, the equipment has been replaced. Since Peter, Paul and Jim bought this equipment from an already operating brewery, they used the setup that was already in place. "We have been operating at a brewery we didn't design," Peter explained.

What is a brewery without a name? At the Portsmouth Brewery in the fall of 1993, there was a staff contest to name the holiday beer that would be brewed. Everyone was invited to vote, and the most popular name would win. The name chosen was Blitzen Ale. Peter wasn't too fond of the name. "It was their contest and their choice, so I had to live with it," he said. One of the names submitted that didn't win was Smuttynose Ale, submitted by a staff member who liked the name because she used to go out to Smuttynose Island and fish with her grandfather as a child. When Peter saw the name, he wasn't familiar with the term, but he learned more about it and wanted to use that name on another beer in the future. A few short months later, that contest entry that didn't win became the name of one of the biggest breweries in New Hampshire.

Paul Murphy, the first brewer at the Portsmouth Brewery, was the first brewer at Smuttynose. Peter also had some of the brewers from the brewery whose equipment he bought join the Smuttynose team. They didn't use any beer recipes from the Portsmouth Brewery. They wanted to separate the identity of Smuttynose and Portsmouth Brewery. "I think we may have done too good of a job because today, many people still don't know the affiliation between Portsmouth and Smuttynose," Peter said. Smuttynose Brewery's flagship beer was Shoals Pale Ale, an American interpretation of an extra special bitter (ESB). Peter had heard about this Redhook Ale Brewery out in Seattle that had an ESB and thought it was a great beer. As you may know, Redhook now has a brewery in New Hampshire, but it didn't then. In the first calendar year, Smuttynose brewed eight hundred barrels of beer. The following year, the barrels were in the thousands. The craft beer scene at the time was growing at a very fast pace, with growth of 50 to 60 percent each year. But it came to a halt in 1996.

Peter explains that from 1996 to 1998, Smuttynose lost 30 percent of its volume. What could be causing this? "The market became very crowded very fast with a lot of brands that weren't craft brands—a lot of light lagers with cute labels. People couldn't distinguish craft beers from these novelty beers," Peter said. Peter was told, "It looks like this craft beer thing has run its course" by wholesalers who feared imported beers would take over, like Bass, Guinness and Heineken, which came into America touting their many centuries of brewing history. This convinced many people that a longer history meant better beer and would stray from those local microbreweries that were starting from scratch. Smuttynose survived this period of unsettling, and then New Hampshire became thirsty. In 2005, the brewery expanded and took over the other half of its Heritage Avenue space, doubling its size to twenty-five thousand square feet. After raising the roof to accommodate two one-hundred-barrel fermenters and adding on to the building, the brewery needed more space. Peter looked into the mills in Newmarket and another space in Portsmouth. Through some more searching, trials and tribulations, it ended up purchasing the fourteen-acre Towle Farm property in Hampton, New Hampshire.

"This building was designed for Towle Farm. A lot of people put a lot of thought into it," Peter said. They broke ground in summer of 2012 with a party of thirsty beer fans, politicians and community members. This massive lot will serve as a brewery complete with tours and growler fills as well as a pub. When you pull into the new facility, you will see an old farmhouse to the right of the main brewery. That farmhouse was initially located right in the middle of the new building. A team of trained professionals moved the building down the hill, where it will become Smuttynose's brewpub.

The entirety of the project, from house moving, building construction and brewing installation, has been captured on camera and can be found on Smuttynose's website.

Everything the team at Smuttynose is doing is to improve the quality of the beer and the workflow for the brewers. At Towle Farm, the brewery has a state-of-the-art brewing system that is nothing like the one at its Heritage Avenue location. Smuttynose wasn't completely in the black when it ordered this new equipment. The cost of the equipment included installation and training. Much of the brewing process here is automated. When brewing beer at such a high scale, breweries are taxed with making it taste the same batch after batch. It is estimated that, in the first year, fifty thousand barrels of beer will be made at the new location. With Smuttynose regularly adding new states to its distribution, it will have plenty of demand to fill. While Smuttynose is putting out a lot of beer, it only represents less than 1 percent of the beer sales in New Hampshire.

Smuttynose brews a lot of barrel-aged beers that can be found in bars across the state. It is the brewery's hope that when it is fully operational at the Towle Farm location that it will keep the Heritage Avenue location for pilot beers and special batches. "I see that facility as having a very long, useful life serving a lot of different purposes," Peter said. Smuttynose has begun to release beers under the name Smuttlabs, as a way to showcase smaller batch–sized beers—beers like the Winter Ale aged in red wine barrels or the Imperial Stout aged in apple brandy oak barrels. One of the more unique creations was with chef Jamie Bissonnette called Pure Biss. This witbier was a cross between the culinary world and the brewing word, using traditional witbier ingredients with kaffir lime leaves, spruce tips and twenty-five pounds of grapefruit zest. By doing these releases, Smuttynose is able to hold on to the audience of beer geeks looking for the next best thing.

Another way to excite beer lovers is the Big Beer Series. Each month, Smuttynose showcases a new beer in its lineup. From the Barleywine to the Baltic Porter and the Farmhouse Ale to the Maibock, they are taking the craft beer community on one tasty journey. The beers are available in stores and select draft lines. If you want to truly celebrate the release of a Big Beer, you can join their club, in which you can preorder your beer each month and celebrate with a gathering at the brewery. Smuttynose is celebrating its twenty-year anniversary in 2014, and it has a lot to celebrate. Raise a glass to one of the oldest breweries in the state!

As you can tell from many chapters in this book, Peter Egelston is one of the most important people in beer in the state of New Hampshire. He was part of a Brewers Guild in his early years with the late Greg Noonan (Seven Barrel Brewery) and Jim Killeen (Nutfield Brewing Company), as well as Scott Rice (Woodstock Brewery). In that time, they changed quite a bit of legislation that has made an impact on the ways breweries operate today: abolishing the 6 percent ABV limit, creating brewery self-distribution and adding retail sales at the brewpub, as well as creating a bill for brewpubs. Brewpubs used to need a brewing license as well as restaurant license; now, the brewpub license combines the two. Peter is happy to see the Granite State Brewers Association being reformed after ten years with a lot of great new breweries taking charge.

# BREWER SPOTLIGHT

## David Yarrington

David Yarrington studied chemistry at Colby College in Waterville, Maine. He spent a summer out in California, where he visited Anchor Brewing Company in San Francisco. At the time, the concept of craft beer was still developing. It was at Anchor where David had his aha moment, while he "was drinking these beautiful beers, fresh from the tap." He returned home to start making his own beers in the 1990s. As a chemistry major, David was fascinated by the science behind home-brewing, and he wanted to learn more about it. He moved back to San Francisco to look for a job in the beer industry. The idea of a career in beer was still a mystery to him: "I didn't know you could have a career doing what you liked to do." He began at the now defunct 20 Tank Brewery before jumping to Colorado's Tommyknocker Brewery. In 1997, David moved across the Pacific to Japan to start Tokyo Brewing Company with his brother, who had been living there at the time. After attempting to open a brewpub, they ended up contracting a beer called Tokyo Ale. The Japanese brewing laws at that time required you to brew a minimum volume in order to obtain a brewer's license. Once the laws changed, small breweries opened all across Japan.

David returned from Japan in 2001, when he joined the UC–Davis Master Brewers Program. Here he spent six months getting every technical question about brewing answered. With his chemistry background, he had a lot of questions, but no one he brewed with had much scientific background at the time. The science of brewing was still quite new for brewers moving up from home-brewing to mass production. Problems could be identified but could not be explained. The library at UC–Davis had texts from the 1800s and other resources that supplied David with the answers he was looking for. After UC–Davis, he was recruited by Peter Egelston for a position at Smuttynose Brewing Company.

When he started, Smuttynose was producing five thousand barrels of beer a year (as opposed to forty-two thousand in 2013). Here, David was able to gain management experience while improving the brewing processes that were in place to make them more efficient: "It's not always about the recipe of the beer. It's about knowing what to do with the equipment and how to identify and fix flaws." He noted the branding was already in the right place for the brewery: "When I showed up at Smuttynose, I was looking at Peter's labels and imagery and branding; they had a handle on that. I was ready to help with the brewing." At the time, Shoals Pale Ale, Old Brown Dog and Robust Porter were the flagship beers. The only recipe Yarrington didn't tweak to make his own was the Old Brown Dog, which was, and still is, a solid brown ale. Shortly after he started, Finestkind IPA was created. At the time, the IPA was still a growing concept in the Northeast. Besides Harpoon IPA, there weren't many local IPAs. Finestkind is currently the biggest seller for Smuttynose and part of the reason for their move to Towle Farm.

Yarrington came in during the start of a plateau in the craft beer industry in New Hampshire (2001–09). Yarrington noted that there was a period where extreme beers were everywhere. An oversaturation of extreme beers make it difficult for someone trying to enter the world of craft beer. Nowadays, even though extreme beers still exist, there is a greater appreciation for simpler beers. "It's nice to see the spectrum of extreme beers being dialed back," Yarrington said. Smuttynose released its Bouncy House Ale in 2013, which, at under 5 percent ABV, can be enjoyed all night. It is these light ABV beers with complex flavors that David hopes to see a resurgence of. He is also looking forward to brewing German styles on their new system at Towle Farm.

David had a unique opportunity to travel to the United Kingdom with Smuttynose's "Minister of Propaganda," John "J.T." Thompson, to the Wadworth Brewery in Devizes. At the time, it was hard to find American craft beer in that area. A pub chain, JD Wetherspoon, had the idea to bring an American craft brewer, Smuttynose, over to brew with local breweries and sell that beer to its pubs.

# 7

# ELM CITY BREWING COMPANY

## 222 WEST STREET #46, KEENE
## (603) 355-3335 | WWW.ELMCITYBREWING.COM |
## FOUNDED 1994

E lm City Brewing Company is the most southwestern brewery of New Hampshire. While Keene isn't a tourist town like Portsmouth, North Conway or Manchester, it is home to many unique shops and Keene State College, which both bring a lot of people through the town. Elm City is one of the oldest brewpubs in the state and is located in a restored mill building, which gives it a great look. Debra Rivest and two friends, brothers Tony and Peter Poanessa, opened Elm City in 1995 as a way to combine their love for home-brewing and food. Tony and Peter took care of the brewing side of the business, and Debra focused on the pub. "Keene was very receptive and enthusiastic while we were planning to open Elm City," Debra said. At the time, the only major brewpub open was Portsmouth Brewery. "People in New Hampshire have always liked beer, but it wasn't as accessible as it was today," she said, referring to the lack of craft breweries in the area. After eight years, Debra became the sole owner of Elm City Brewing Company. Peter continued to work at his sign-making company, Keene Signworx. To this day, you can still see signs made by Peter up and down the streets of Keene and scattered about New Hampshire. Debra describes it as an outdoor art gallery for Peter's sign business.

On the brewing side of the house, Elm City has a seven-barrel system and is led by Ben Mullett. Ben was an assistant for many years but has been the head brewer since 2012. When Ben took over, he made the recipes his own. Standard mainstay beers like their Keene Kolsch and fruit beers Peachy Keene and Raspberry Wheat (both made from the Kolsch) have been

Elm City Brewing Company in Keene, New Hampshire. *Photo courtesy of Brian Aldrich.*

Elm City taps on display in Keene, New Hampshire. *Photo courtesy of Brian Aldrich.*

revamped to Ben's liking. You are more than likely to find those three beers always on tap. Other beers include, well, anything under the sun. "I love brewing many different beers. In 2013, I brewed forty different recipes," Ben said with a huge smile on his face. He truly is in a playground of beer recipes and loves tweaking recipes to see how ingredients integrate with one another. Some locals even bring Ben homegrown hops, which he adds as finishing, aroma hops in some of his beers. While Debra owns the establishment, there is a great trustworthy owner/brewer relationship going on, and the locals are loving the beers coming to the taps at Elm City.

The food has a local focus, and that's all because of Debra. From getting local food from farmers and running farmers' markets at Elm City's location, Debra ensures you will have fresh food when you dine here. Debra could run for mayor of Keene if she wanted to. Her focus on keeping a green footprint at the brewery by taking various environmental measures and her love for the community shows she is going far beyond the role of a business owner. "If someone in the area is in need, I want to help them," Debra said. "I like to raise money for charities, schools, animal rights, community kitchens—anything that will help the community."

This sense of community goes for the beer community, too. When you walk into the pub, you will see growlers lining the walls, all from different

Elm City Brewing Company in Keene, New Hampshire. *Photo courtesy of Elm City Brewing Company.*

breweries in the country. They also have a mug club, much like many other breweries in New Hampshire, which hang above the bar. Each year, Elm City hosts a beer tasting dinner for which they invite other brewers to come down with their beer and talk to beer lovers in an intimate setting. Breweries include some mentioned in this book (Martha's Exchange, Flying Goose and Schilling, among others) as well as Massachusetts breweries Amherst Brewing Company and People's Pint, among others. The theme throughout the craft beer scene is camaraderie, and Elm City showcases it as much as it can. If you are given the opportunity to travel to Keene, we highly recommend you stop in and grab some food and beer from Elm City Brewing Company.

# 8

# SEVEN BARREL BREWERY

## 5 AIRPORT ROAD, WEST LEBANON (603) 298-5566 | WWW.7BARREL.COM | FOUNDED 1994

I f you were to throw a dart at a map of Vermont and New Hampshire, a bulls-eye would put you at Seven Barrel Brewery in West Lebanon, New Hampshire. At the crossroad of Routes 91 and 89, Seven Barrel is a spot for people traveling up to Vermont or down through New Hampshire but also has a big local following. The brewery's ties to Vermont and New Hampshire go far beyond just being in the middle of both states. In 1994, the late Greg Noonan, a legend from the craft beer uprising in New England, opened Seven Barrel Brewery as a sister brewery to his Vermont Pub and Brewery, which opened in 1988 and is located in downtown Burlington, Vermont. While both brewpubs have a similar feel, they are different in customer attraction. Burlington is a tourist town, and West Lebanon is not. Seven Barrel thrives off the locals and is focused on keeping them happy while also trying to attract beer geeks on a beer adventure.

Tony Lubold started as a home-brewer and is now the brew master at Seven Barrel, which not coincidentally is a seven-barrel brewing system. Tony started at the now defunct Catamount Brewery in 1989, a brewery where Tod Mott, ex-brewer of Portsmouth Brewery was an apprentice. In 2000, Catamount Brewery went up for sale and was purchased by Harpoon. The Windsor, Vermont Harpoon brewery now stands here and can be visited year round. Tony received awards in national home-brew competitions for his lager beers. Seven Barrel's standard year-round selections include Cream Ale, Dublin Brown, Red #7 Red Ale, Champagne Reserve IPA and Oatmeal Stout. "Cream Ale is a good start for those new to craft beer; then head to the Red #7—it's a mild beer, not very hoppy. It is our most popular beer," Tony said. Tony enjoys IPAs and states they are being requested all the time at the pub. As a nod to local agriculture, Tony gets hops for special batch experiments from the Addison Hop Farm in Addison, Vermont.

Due to their seasonal tourist attraction, Tony mainly brews the beers the locals enjoy because they are his best customers. The brew house and the fermenters are on opposite sides of the pub, a setup that allows Tony to see and talk with customers regularly when brewing. Many of New Hampshire's breweries' serving tanks are out of sight, but not at Seven Barrel. The serving tanks are right behind the bar, which gives those at the bar a real sense for how much beer is brewed at the brewery. Tony has tastings with the staff so they can give the customers an accurate description of the beer. Teaching your staff about beer if you own a brewery, restaurant or bar is a vital piece of the craft beer puzzle that many fail at. It is as simple as being able to describe the flavor, style and bitterness of a beer. This will allow someone new to craft beer to not feel intimidated.

Although the only place where you can purchase Seven Barrel beer is at the brewery, you can find Tony at brew fests across New England, including the great Passport event at Portsmouth's Strawbery Banke Museum. Each year, Strawbery Banke hosts this "Craft Beer and Culinary World Tour" on their grounds. The concept is simple and complex at the same time. Breweries are selected to pour beer at the event and are randomly paired up with top chefs from the seacoast. The event sells out every year, and the line to get in wraps around the museum. During the event last year, the museum had resident cooper Ron Raiselis making barrels on site as well as other attractions to show off Strawbery Banke's focus on history.

Fun Fact: *Smuttynose Brewery brewed a beer called Noonan in honor of the late Greg Noonan. The black IPA is now bottled and available late between late winter and early summer. Black IPA is a style of beer that originated at Noonan's Vermont brewpub back in 1994.*

# 9
# WOODSTOCK INN STATION & BREWERY

## 135 MAIN STREET, NORTH WOODSTOCK
## (603) 745-3951 | WWW.WOODSTOCKINNBREWERY.COM |
## FOUNDED 1995

The Woodstock Inn Station & Brewery is located in scenic North Woodstock, New Hampshire, within the White Mountain Range. This location is truly an outdoorsman's paradise. Whether it is the dead of winter or the middle of summer, there is always something to do in this area. Winter sports lovers can take in the breathtaking mountains via skiing, snowboarding, snowshoeing or even snowmobiling on one of the hundreds of trails that snake through the White Mountains. The White Mountains are a short drive at less than two hours in the car if you are traveling from the seacoast region.

The White Mountains themselves are a large mountain range that covers about a quarter of New Hampshire and even a little piece of western Maine. Most famous of these mountains is Mount Washington, which stands 6,288 feet. It is not only the tallest of the White Mountains but also the highest peak in northeastern United States. Many people flock to hike this mountain in the summertime, as well as other mountains that line the Presidential Mountain Range. There is a breathtaking array of scenery within these mountains, which are home to beautiful waterfalls and tree views that overlook the Granite State that will stick with you forever. A piece of advice to those looking to hike Mount Washington: Devote a whole day to the hike. It is a beautiful, challenging hike that should be enjoyed to the fullest. If you don't fancy yourself a hiker, the summit can be reached via an access road where cars are allowed to drive to the top, but where is the fun in that? Strap on your pack and get on the trail!

Mount Tecumseh trees. *Photo courtesy of Corey O'Connor, www.coreyoconnorphoto.com.*

If you are a hiker, camper or just an all-around outdoorsman, there are plenty of places to set up camp along Interstate 93. To those that are more adventurous, you can stay in one of the eight High Huts. These huts are owned and operated by the Appalachian Mountain Club, whose huts are located along the Appalachian Trail. In the summer months, those hiking the mountain trails can benefit from "full services" that include meals and a place to lay your head at night that isn't in a tent. You have to book these ahead of time—so don't expect to be able to drop in, or you will be sleeping in the trees! These huts are positioned in gorgeous locations along the trails and are great spots to stop and grab some water and a few pictures of this beautiful part of New England. We highly recommend taking a few days to hike and explore the White Mountains. You won't be disappointed.

Once you are done exploring the mountain and are ready to come down, we highly recommend a stop at the Woodstock Inn Station & Brewery. This location has been a longtime watering hole for hikers, skiers and locals living in the mountain range. The Woodstock Inn is a brewpub and full-scale brewery that captures that true New England vibe. Every wall is lined with signs, photos and even a few stuffed animals that give you the ski lodge feel. A large roaring fireplace is the feature point in the main bar area when you first walk through the doors.

The Woodstock Station was originally the Lincoln Railroad Station, which was constructed in the late 1800s. This location has always been bustling and has seen tremendous growth throughout the years. In the mid-'30s and '40s, ski traffic brought tourists by the trainload from Boston and New York City to the mountain region to hit the slopes. As the years pressed on, expansion brought the creation of the Woodstock Inn brewery and brewpub. At the time, this seven-barrel brewing facility brewed crowd favorites like Pigs Ear Brown Ale (4.3 percent ABV, medium bodied brown ale with a smooth finish) and Old Man Oatmeal Stout (5.13 percent ABV, creamy unfiltered oatmeal stout with roasted and black patent malt). The creation of the Woodstock Inn Station & Brewery has put North Woodstock on the map as the spot to visit when traveling the mountains of New Hampshire.

The Woodstock Station Restaurant is filled with high-top tables in the main bar area. If you are looking for a more quiet dining experience, there is a small dining room off to the side that will allow you to enjoy a somewhat quiet meal with family and friends. The menu is chock-full of great choices ranging from traditional appetizers, such as the chicken wings, to the more exotic "Fiery Frogs Legs." The main courses are hearty and filling, and there are plenty to choose from. Those who like variety will truly enjoy this menu. Personally, we recommend the Spicy Mac & Cheese. You won't be disappointed. Don't be afraid to start your day here either. The Woodstock Station Restaurant has one of the best breakfast menus in the mountains. Try the grits. Trust us.

The brewpub is one of the best parts of the trip. Modeled after a traditional English pub, this cozy space allows you to eat, drink and be merry with your friends. While enjoying a pint or two, you can view the original seven-barrel system that is still used today right off the brewpub. The friendly and knowledgeable waitstaff will help you select the perfect pint. If you are having trouble selecting, try a sampler of five of their beers. It's the perfect way to try them all.

This location offers a charming atmosphere that many couples looking to get married love. The weddings at the Woodstock Inn are held in their hall on the second floor, and it is as busy as ever. Book early if you are thinking about celebrating your nuptials at this brewery. The balcony off the hall overlooks a neighboring church that defines that small-town New England feel. If you time it just right, you may be able to catch the sun setting over the town of North Woodstock.

The team at the Woodstock Inn works to offer you a variety of things such as a private bar, a large stage and even your own custom labels on the bottles for the party! The crew at the inn will work with you to customize the labels so your guests can enjoy a tasty brew with your face on it—or anything you want for that matter. What better way to enjoy a beer than with you or your loved one's face on the bottle?

The second-floor location allows for privacy in a very public setting. On any given weekend during the winter or summer months, the bar, restaurant and brewpub are packed with visitors looking to get their hands on one of the many beers brewed and distributed on site.

Lodging is always a key element to any trip, and the Woodstock Inn has you covered with a variety of locations to stay in. Each location within the Woodstock Inn network has a tremendous amount of charm, and you will surely be able to relax and enjoy all that North Woodstock has to offer. Be sure to check out their accommodation packages, which include a "Brewer's Weekend" package. This package allows you to stay at the inn and learn the brewing experience on site with the crew of Woodstock Inn's brewery. It is a truly unique experience that allows you to see a side of brewing and beer that not many people can witness. This unique atmosphere will surely brighten up your trip to the mountains if you decide to stay at the Woodstock Inn.

The Woodstock Inn's brewery is truly two breweries in one, a combination of the original seven-barrel system established in 1996 and its new state-of-the-art thirty-barrel system created in 2012. It is at this location where the beer is brewed, bottled and prepped for distribution through the New England region. The Woodstock Inn's brewery provides its beer in kegs and twelve- and twenty-two-ounce bottles for the public to enjoy. With well over a dozen beers, the brewery focuses on consistency in its brews. It prides itself on high-quality, delicious beers that people will enjoy time and time again. As far as craft breweries go, it has got its processes down to a science.

While touring the mountains, we had the pleasure of getting a tour of this facility from Garrett Smith, brewery sales representative for the Woodstock Inn Station & Brewery, who showed us the inner workings of the brewery. This location is the perfect combination of old-school brewing and brewing in the modern age. The seven-barrel system just off the brewpub is a testament to how the brewery got its route in the craft market. Still in use today, this system was up and running the day we toured the facility and is still used to brew on a regular basis. The gorgeous brick-and-copper kettle catches your attention and is a beautiful piece of brewing machinery.

A few short steps outside led us to a bulkhead door to the basement. At first glance, it doesn't look like much, but after venturing down below, we

At the mash tun with Errol "Butch" Chase, brewer at Woodstock Inn Station & Brewery.
*Photo courtesy of Scott Rice.*

were able to see their grundy tanks up close and personal. This system is a proven workhorse for the brewery that still assists in providing beer to the general public who are looking to drink in the brewpub. From here, we made our way over to the expansion portion of the brewery. Upon walking through the doors, you are met by dozens of pallets filled with product awaiting distribution to the New England region. As mentioned earlier, this thirty-barrel system was created in 2012 and has helped the Woodstock Inn's brewery team meet its growing demand in the region. The brewery provides a wide array of beers to its markets. In regards to its seasonal offerings, its autumnal beer Autumn Ale Brew goes against the ever-popular pumpkin flavor and offers a fresh, crisp medium-bodied ale with light hints of apple and cinnamon. Hats off to Errol "Butch" Chase, head brewer at the Woodstock Inn Station & Brewery, and the rest of the team. They are doing amazing things and are ready to welcome you in after a long day of seeing the sights. If you are up in the area during the fall, stop in after gazing at the autumn foliage for one of these incredible brews on tap.

The tour was incredibly educational, offering a healthy balance of beer knowledge and cool facts about the location in North Woodstock, New Hampshire. Culture and hospitality have developed this location into the landmark it is today. Owner Scott Rice has worked with his team to create a destination that visitors will want to visit over and over throughout the years.

## History

In 2013, Governor Maggie Hassan held a bill-signing ceremony at the Woodstock Inn that would help change the craft brewing industry in New Hampshire. The bill revised NH RSA 178:12-A (the nanobrewery license) to allow and establish limitations on sales of beer by nanobreweries for consumption on premise. To commemorate the signing, the Woodstock brewery team created a special "Maggie Hassan Edition" of its Celebration Ale, which featured the governor on the label of the bottle. This bill helped push the growth of the craft movement in the state of New Hampshire, and the Woodstock Inn Station & Brewery is pleased to be a part of that momentous day in craft brewing history.

As mentioned earlier in this chapter, this location has a gorgeous landscape that should be explored at great length. Be sure to carve out a long weekend to take in all that the White Mountains have to offer. This area provides countless activities and is filled with amazing people who welcome visitors in with open arms. If you play your cards right, they will give you some pointers on local trails, events and even their favorite place to grab a cold pint.

# 10

# REDHOOK ALE BREWERY

1 REDHOOK WAY PEASE INTERNATIONAL TRADEPORT, PORTSMOUTH
(603) 430-8600 | WWW.REDHOOK.COM |
FOUNDED 1996

D riving through the Portsmouth traffic circle, you begin to smell what beer geeks would say is the best smell in the world: beer being brewed. Follow that smell a couple miles, and you will end up at the biggest craft brewery in New Hampshire, Redhook Ale Brewery. Redhook started in Seattle, Washington, in 1981 and opened its pub and brewing facility in 1994 in Woodinville, Washington. In 1996, a second Redhook brewing facility was built on the Pease International Tradeport in Portsmouth. One of the main components in finding a second Redhook location was matching the water quality that the current operating brewery had. After researching, the brewers found that there are a lot of matching qualities between Northwest and Northeast water. Surprisingly, when they started brewing at Pease, they ended up with base water and not city water as they originally thought they would get. Every day for the first year, a tanker truck would drive up to a water tower to get city water and bring it to the brewery for brewing operations. Much like a lot of big breweries, Redhook now has its own in-house water treatment program that allows them to get the water pH balance to their liking and make it identical to their Northwest brewery. Brewing with the same water quality is crucial not just when having two breweries but also when wanting to put out a consistent product. Once the Portsmouth Redhook Ale Brewery was up and running, the two breweries would meet on a regular basis for quality control on their year-round beers. The Portsmouth Redhook brewery distributes east of the Mississippi, and Woodinville takes the west. While the brewing systems in both locations

Redhook Brewery Long Hammer neon sign. *Photo courtesy of Carla Companion.*

are very high tech, when you have over two dozen brewers across both locations, you will have different styles and techniques of brewing that need to be baselined to make the same beers taste the same. The most popular Redhook beer is the Longhammer IPA, which can be found on nearly every beer store shelf in America. Other highlights include their ESB, Blackhook and Audible Ale.

One of the biggest fun facts you may not know at first glance is that there is more than just Redhook beer being brewed at the brewery in Portsmouth. In 2008, Widmer Brothers Brewing out of Portland, Oregon, merged with Redhook, forming what is now called the Craft Brew Alliance, also known as the CBA. The alliance focuses on being able to distribute more beer to more people across the country. Widmer beer is now being brewed at Redhook breweries. In 2010, the CBA added Kailua-Kona, Hawaii's Kona Brewing Company to the portfolio, which is also being brewed on Redhook's 180,000-barrel system. Turns out, Widmer Hefeweizen was the top-selling beer at the Redhook brewery in Portsmouth when the CBA was formed. Being able to introduce many different varieties of beer to the consumer is great for customer retention and also makes it fun for the brewers. Over a

BREWING FROM SEA TO SUMMIT

Tanks at Redhook Brewery located in Portsmouth, New Hampshire. *Photo courtesy of Carla Companion.*

dozen brewers work around the clock to produce these beers. Now when you visit the pub, you will see around fifteen taps of Redhook, Widmer and Kona beers that change regularly. Due to the size and age of Redhook compared to the newer craft brewers in New Hampshire, one would think Redhook needed to reformulate to adjust to the growing popularity of craft beer, but think again. The response to Redhook beer in 1996 is the same as it is today, which is great. To mix things up for the brewers, there is a separate three-barrel system in the brewery for them to create whatever beer they want. This is called the Pease Project. This gives the brewers the opportunity to showcase their talents by producing beers only poured at the pub and limited tap handles in Portsmouth. If there was ever doubt in the ability of brewers who brew beer on such a mass scale, you should see what they are doing at the Redhook brewery.

Just like any other brewery, Redhook creates waste during its production process. Waste is accumulated in the form of old aluminum kegs, low-density polyethylene (LDPE) keg caps, cardboard boxes and green polyethylene terephthalate (PET) strapping. But what makes Redhook special when it comes to waste is its "sustainable recycling" efforts. Three years ago, Redhook was working with an average waste-hauling company that did exactly that, hauled the brewery's waste away, most often to a landfill. Unsatisfied with this solution, Redhook began working with the recycling company Poly Recovery, a pioneer in sustainable, locally based, full-service recycling. Poly Recovery is able to find solutions for all waste streams, specializing in plastic waste, which the company processes and transforms into an end-user-ready regrind for local manufacturers. Since working with Poly Recovery, Redhook has replaced the catch-all compactor and all four dumpsters around its facility, saving $3,000 a month on hauling fees and preventing ten thousand pounds of waste from going to a landfill on a monthly basis. By providing traceability and asking, "Where does our waste go?" Redhook has found an environmentally, socially and financially sustainable solution to its waste.

Redhook is also home to two large events, the New Hampshire Brewfest in the fall and Redhook Fest in the summer. The brewfest brings together forty breweries from across the country pouring over 150 beers on the grounds of Redhook. Breweries are excited to come to this festival because of the popularity and uniqueness. Bands play on a stage, and food is served from local restaurants. New Hampshire is home to many great festivals, and this is one of the greats. Redhook hosts its own festival every year known as the Redhook Fest. Redhook Fest is for music and beer lovers. Every summer, a popular band is brought in to play and attendees are encouraged to bring their lawn chairs and relax while drinking great beer.

Food doesn't play second fiddle to the beer at Redhook. Great pub food is served in the Cataqua Public House, named after the Piscataqua River, which runs through Maine and New Hampshire. Weddings, company events, parties and celebrations of the like are held all the time in the Ale Maker's Hall. To celebrate its thirty-year anniversary in 2011, Redhook turned part of Ale Maker's Hall into a man cave complete with poker tables, big screen televisions and beef jerky. Don't pass up the opportunity for a tour of the facility, which runs daily. A tour ends with beer samples if that helps persuade you.

# 11

# FLYING GOOSE BREW PUB

## 40 ANDOVER ROAD, NEW LONDON
## (603) 526-6899 | WWW.FLYINGGOOSE.COM |
## FOUNDED 1996

C raft brewing is a simple, dedicated art. The majority of people involved in this industry are in it for the love of the beer. Beer is a common bond that holds these individuals together. Some would go as far as to call the craft beer community in New Hampshire a family. This theme rings out loud and clear at the Flying Goose Brew Pub. From the moment you walk into this small building just off Route 89 in New London, New Hampshire, you are welcomed in by the atmosphere. The sense of history and togetherness draws you in. Combine this feeling with a gorgeous view of the New Hampshire countryside, and you have what we like to call in the industry a "package deal." The Flying Goose Brew Pub was established in 1993, but the building has been a part of the New London community for quite some time. This establishment is located at the Crockett's Corner in New London, New Hampshire, on the corner of Route 11 and Route 114. People in this community have long referred to this area of New Hampshire as the feel good spot of New London. Over the years, it has housed everything from ice cream shops to the now infamous Flying Goose Brew Pub.

The building that houses this seasoned brewpub is filled with things that embody the spirit of comfort. Rich dark wood tones decorate the bar while antique metal tackers line the walls around you. The majority of the back wall of the restaurant is windows. This was done to show people the beauty of the landscape surrounding this establishment. Its beauty is not only enjoyed but also harvested and utilized by the Flying Goose. One of the many policies owner and founder Tom Millis has put into place here at the Flying Goose is one of environmental responsibility. Tom took it upon himself to bring his business into the twenty-first century in regard to waste management, power and heat. We were honored to receive a tour of the facility during which Tom himself showed us his pride and joy.

Tom Millis prides himself on the business he has built. He understands that to create something amazing like a restaurant or a brewery, you have to be smart with how you manage your business. Heavy focus on cost reduction in day-to-day practices helps keep the Flying Goose on track. Providing a comfortable, unique dining experience and creating quality, delicious beers for the community is the overall goal. Managing your business tightly and in an effective manner keeps the brewpub on top.

Priding itself on being the first brewery in New Hampshire to harness solar power, the Flying Goose taps into many energy-efficient resources to fuel its day-to-day operations, including pellet stoves and high-tech, energy-efficient fans that seal or release heat effectively. One of the biggest, and most notable, landmarks at the facility is the rows and rows of solar panels. Lining the back property, 180 solar panels work to store energy and fuel the Flying Goose. It's a gorgeous site that shows the future of energy efficiency in the craft brewing community.

Expansion is the plan for the future at the Flying Goose. It will expand into its parking lot a bit to include official grain storage, cold storage for kegs and other brewery-related items. The expansion is necessary to help foster the growth of the brewery and help bring more of its beer to the community, but more importantly, it will allow the brewery to store beer more efficiently so none goes to waste over time. It's another example of working smarter, not harder, at the brewpub. However, an amazing example of working hard is embodied in the brewery's head brewer, Rik Marley. We had the unique, and backbreaking, experience of meeting with Rik on a brew day. This is what happened next.

We were introduced to Rik during the middle of one of his brews, a honey ale. He welcomed us into his very crowded, cramped and bustling brewery with a sense of belonging. The facility is crammed wall to wall with mash tuns, fermentation tanks, casks and other brewing paraphernalia. Most people would be claustrophobic, but Rik's persona truly puts you at ease. There were a few moments of pleasantries before he jumped into the brewing scene in New Hampshire. Rik reiterated to us what we have heard from dozens of craft brewers before him: "It's insane how many breweries are in planning just in New Hampshire…it's a crazy time for the craft beer industry."

Rik Marley discussing beer while brewing. *Photo courtesy of Michael Meredith.*

Rik started at Flying Goose on September 1, 2009. However, his first job as a brewer was at the Woodstock Inn Station & Brewery in Woodstock, New Hampshire, which he started in 2004. Before he started full time at Flying Goose, Rik was brewing for two breweries in 2008–09, the Woodstock Inn and Italian Oasis Brewing in Littleton, New Hampshire. At Italian Oasis, Rik was able to start experimenting with brews of his own and putting in countless hours of brewing. He was literally working seven days a week as a brewer and developing his mark in the brewing world. Once he started working at the Flying Goose, Rik was prepped and ready to take on brewing solo. His interest in brewing didn't develop in the year 2004; it had started long before that in the '90s, when he began brewing where most brewers start—at home.

The scene is Rob's Homebrew Shop in Concord, New Hampshire, where Rik uttered the words that all beer lovers utter at some point in their beer-drinking careers: "Man, it would be awesome to make your own beer!" After enjoying a few beers, he was interrupted by the owner of Rob's Homebrew and taken to the back to view all the home-brewing equipment. It was that year, for either his birthday or Christmas (he couldn't quite recall), that he received his first home-brewing kit, and from that point on, it was all brewing all the time.

Within a few days of receiving this kit, he was brewing his first IPA. Using his friends as testers, Rik began to crave brewing more and more. Over time, he collected countless books on brewing and began to pick the brains of people in the beer community. Anything that could help him get better at brewing, he was doing it. Living in Idaho at the time, Rik used to follow the band Phish on tour, and while he was touring the country after the band, he started selling home-brews out of his van. It was on these tours that he developed the nickname "the home-brew guy." Known to all as the dude selling quality brews out of his van, Rik quickly gained popularity, and because of that, he began to sell more and more beer. After a successful run of selling every single one of the brews he produced for the tour at a Phil & Friends show in California at the Greek Theater in Berkeley, he started to realize that this could be his calling.

Throughout his brewing career, Rik has taken his positive attitude to everything he does. He is a ball of energy that stopped twice the entire time we were with him. The first time was to hand us a beer, and the second was to hand us a shovel to start scooping out the mash tun once his brew was complete. He wanted us to experience what it was like to be brewers. It's not all about standing around and drinking beer. It's backbreaking work that isn't for the faint of heart. At the end of the day, it is a combination of manufacturing, art and brute strength. Rik embodies hard work and originality in his day-to-day life. We were honored to brew and share a pint with him.

The crew at the Flying Goose serves a wide variety of beers at its restaurant, not just its own. The brewery wants people to come in and have the beer that they want. However, the Flying Goose team takes a tremendous amount of pride in the beers it brews and will do its best to get you to try something outside your comfort zone by allowing you to sample its large array of brews.

Flying Goose is constantly brewing up new beers, but we were able to sample a few of the brewery's staples, as well as a few of its specialties. The specialty beer at the time was a Valentine's Day specific beer— Chocolate Milk Stout, a smooth, creamy stout that is brewed with organic Madagascar vanilla beans and organic Ecuadorian cocoa nibs. Rik allowed us to taste it straight from the barrel, and it was truly a delight. While we helped him brew, Rik presented us with his pride and joy, the Long Brothers American-style IPA. This full bodied, rich in taste India pale ale is a strong, well-balanced brew that goes down easy. As Rik would say, it is "intense but not obnoxious."

Flying Goose Brew Pub hallway wall hangings. *Photo courtesy of Michael Meredith.*

Flying Goose Brew Pub sign. *Photo courtesy of Michael Meredith.*

At one point, the Flying Goose was a seasonal establishment, but an increase in traffic throughout all the seasons has allowed it to stay busy year round. In the winter, the ski crowd floods into its establishment throughout the week. Mere minutes from great skiing at Sunapee, the Flying Goose is the place to go after you are done hitting the slopes. The summer months bring in sightseers from all over the Northeast who are looking to take in the absolute beauty of New Hampshire's mountain ranges.

The staff members at the Flying Goose prides themselves on their hospitality. Rik, Tom and the rest of the crew truly pulled out the red carpet for us, and they will for you, too. Be sure to stop in and see them on your next trip to New Hampshire, and don't forget to take in the scenery.

*Above*: Wood-fire oven at Schilling Beer Company. *Photo courtesy of Schilling Beer Company.*

*Left*: John Lenzini, head brewer of Schilling Brewery. *Photo courtesy of Schilling Beer Company.*

Moat Iron Mike cans on the line. *Photo courtesy of Bill Lee.*

Fear No Beer kegs. *Photo courtesy of Michael Meredith.*

*Above*: A selection of pints at Woodstock Inn Station & Brewery. *Photo courtesy of Michael Meredith.*

*Right*: A bottle of 603 Brewery's 18 Mile Ale at the beach. *Photo courtesy of Tamsin Hewes.*

Blue Lobster tap handles at WHYM Craft Beer Café. *Photo courtesy of Michael Meredith.*

New Hampshire waterfall. *Photo courtesy of Corey O'Connor, www.coreyoconnorphoto.com.*

Hiker on a frozen lake. *Photo courtesy of Corey O'Connor, www.coreyoconnorphoto.com.*

View from Mount Lafayette. *Photo courtesy of Corey O'Connor, www.coreyoconnorphoto.com.*

Portsmouth Brewery pint. *Photo courtesy of Corey O'Connor, www.coreyoconnorphoto.com.*

Redhook Brewery welcome hall. *Photo courtesy of Redhook Brewery.*

Flying Goose hop fields. *Photo courtesy of Rik Marley.*

Brian helping with the brewing of a golden ale at Flying Goose Brew Pub. *Photo courtesy of Michael Meredith.*

Martha's Exchange brewing facility. *Photo courtesy of Michael Meredith.*

Greg, head brewer of Martha's Exchange. *Photo courtesy of Michael Meredith.*

*Above*: Martha's Exchange
candy counter. *Photo courtesy of
Michael Meredith.*

*Right*: White Birch
Brewing's Belgian-style
IPA. *Photo courtesy of White
Birch Brewing.*

Bill Herlicka, founder of White Birch Brewing. *Photo courtesy of White Birch Brewing.*

Valley Malt hop fields in Hadley, Massachusetts. *Photo courtesy of Andrea Stanley.*

*Above*: Annette Lee of
Throwback Brewery with
mash tun. *Photo courtesy of
Throwback Brewery*.

*Right*: Seven Barrel Brewery.
*Photo courtesy of Jason Phelps*.

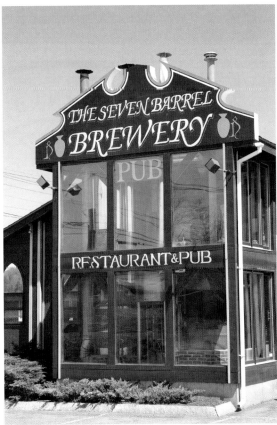

FINESTKIND IPA

*"India Pale Ale."*                    *"Finestkind."*

BREWED & BOTTLED BY SMUTTYNOSE BREWING COMPANY, HAMPTON, NH, USA          12 FL OZ/355ML

THE FLYING GOOSE ◆ BREW PUB & GRILLE

*Opposite, top*: Smuttynose Brewing Company Finestkind label. *Photo courtesy of Smuttynose Brewing Company.*

*Opposite, bottom*: Flying Goose Brew Pub logo. *Photo courtesy of Flying Goose Brew Pub.*

*Right*: Throwback Brewery's Maple-kissed Wheat Porter. *Photo courtesy of Throwback Brewery.*

*Below*: A sample at Earth Eagle Brewings in Portsmouth, New Hampshire. *Photo courtesy of Carla Companion.*

Lighthouse off the coast of Portsmouth, New Hampshire. *Photo courtesy of Corey O'Connor, www.coreyoconnorphoto.com.*

Anheuser-Busch Clydesdales. *Photo courtesy of Scott Louis Photography, http://swlouis.com.*

Mike Mooney and John Pelech of Poly Recovery in Portsmouth, New Hampshire. *Photo courtesy of Poly Recovery.*

Frank Jones Brewery & Malt House in Portsmouth, New Hampshire. *Photo courtesy of Library of Congress, LC-DIG-pga-00376.*

Ben Mullett, head brewer at Elm City Brewing Company in Keene, New Hampshire. *Photo courtesy of Elm City Brewing Company.*

White Mountains landscape. *Photo courtesy of Corey O'Connor, www.coreyoconnorphoto.com.*

12

# TUCKERMAN BREWING COMPANY

## 64 HOBBS STREET, CONWAY
## (603) 447-5400 | WWW.TUCKERMANBREWING.COM |
## FOUNDED 1998

Northern New Hampshire is busy year round. Whether you are hiking or skiing, there is a good chance you are passing through Conway. It is up here where one of the most recognizable breweries of New Hampshire is located—Tuckerman Brewing Company. Started by Kirsten Neve and Nik Stanciu in 1998, Tuckerman is a brewery you need to see to believe. From the second you walk into the brewery on Hobbs Street in Conway, you will be looking for the rest of it. From a beer geek's perspective, it is amazing how such a relatively small-looking brewery can be distributing as much beer as it does. You will be hard-pressed not to find Tuckerman on draft or bottled at a bar in each town in New Hampshire. It's that type of voodoo magic that makes Tuckerman's worth seeking out. Currently producing eight thousand barrels of beer a year, Kristen, Nik and their team of brewers are working long, hard hours to put out a solid lineup of beers.

Tuckerman Brewing Company currently produces three styles throughout the year (Pale Ale, Headwall Alt and Altitude) and one seasonal (6288 Stout) to keep up with demand. The Pale Ale is the flagship for Tuckerman and is a beer you can drink any time of year, whether it be after mowing your lawn or at the end of long day of skiing. The Headwall Alt is an altbier, a German brown ale with a great malt flavor. Tuckerman is the only brewery in the state producing an altbier year round. You can also find a kicked-up version of the brewery's Headwall Alt called Altitude (an altbier with attitude). Finally, its winter seasonal, 6288 Stout, is named for the tallest

Pallet of kegs at the Tuckerman Brewing Company. *Photo courtesy of Michael Meredith.*

peak in New Hampshire, Mount Washington. Rightfully so, on a cold winter night after hiking, skiing or shopping in the Conway area, you should be reaching for a stout like 6288. Tuckerman's artwork features photos from the various ski trails and mountains from the area, a visual you won't see from many other breweries in the state. The same goes for the brewery. When you tour Tuckerman Brewing Company, you will notice photos plastered all over the taproom that show fans with Tuckerman beer on various hiking or ski trails all over the state.

There are a lot of breweries in this book with a vast array of beers. Tuckerman's has kept it extremely simple by only producing the above four beers. We have been to many breweries where a beer drinker will say "Is this all you have?" or "You don't have this style?" You don't hear complaints about Tuckerman. The universal rule in brewing—whether at a just-started nanobrewery or at place that has been around for years—is "consistency is key." If the beer you are producing cannot be consistent from batch to batch, you need to reassess your system. For sixteen years, Tuckerman has hit the nail on the head with its Pale Ale. There are plans for expansion across the street from the current location. This will allow the brewery to produce more of its current lineup, as well as introduce new beers to its catalogue. For now, you can visit the current location for a tour and beer samples or pick up Tuckerman's beer all across the state.

# THE NEW ENGLAND BREWFEST

Among all the beer festivals across New England where you will find Tuckerman pouring the brewery's beer, the New England Brewfest is one of the biggest. Celebrating its tenth year in June 2014, the New England Brewfest is an entire weekend of beer-related events held in Lincoln, New Hampshire. From keynote speeches to panel discussions and workshops to homebrew demos, this is no ordinary festival. You can choose to attend all of the events or just come to the Saturday night festival, which highlights breweries from around New England. The weekend closes with a farewell tour at Woodstock Brewery. There is no better way to try to cram in as much beer-centric activities along with the beautiful sights of the mountains than the New England Brewfest.

# 13
# MOAT MOUNTAIN SMOKEHOUSE & BREWING COMPANY

## 3378 WHITE MOUNTAIN HIGHWAY, NORTH CONWAY (603) 356-6381 | WWW.MOATMOUNTAIN.COM | FOUNDED 2000

The mountain region of New Hampshire is a beautiful place on many levels. Whether it's from seeing the gorgeous mountain ranges or meeting the amazing people, you are going to feel at home wherever you go. There is plenty to do and lots to see, but we recommend you take some time to mingle with the locals and get to know the story from them. Everywhere we went in the mountains, we asked the people where they like to drink, what they like to drink and, of course, why do they drink it?

When we rolled into the town of North Conway in the dead of winter, we were surrounded by skiers, snowboarders and ice climbers. This small ski town located in the center of New Hampshire just moments away from the Maine border has a lot to offer in regards to tourism and hospitality. This town is literally packed with people in the winter and summer months, but it is not an overwhelming crowd. Right from the start, we could tell we were going to enjoy the atmosphere of a bustling town, and we weren't disappointed.

The North Conway area is an outdoorsman's dream. Located in the White Mountains, there is plenty of skiing and snowboarding to take part in. Cranmore Mountain Resort is located in North Conway and is a popular spot for people to hit the slopes. In the summer and autumn months, taking a drive on the scenic Kancamagus Highway is a gorgeous way to see New Hampshire's beauty. Spanning thirty-four miles from North Conway to Lincoln, this road is littered with waterfalls, trails and other scenic points

Life Is Short—Drink Good Beer. *Photo courtesy of Michael Meredith.*

along the way. Before you go leaving town though, there is one place that you absolutely must visit if you consider yourself a craft beer lover—Moat Mountain Smokehouse & Brewery.

The crew at Moat Mountain Smokehouse & Brewery redefines the words "culture" and "togetherness." Established in 2000, Moat Mountain Smokehouse was founded by Stephen Johnson and Vicky Valentino, who began envisioning the restaurant and brewery after acquiring the property in the late 1990s. With a strong background in culinary arts, Stephen and Vicky were looking to bring a unique dining experience for the patrons who attended Moat Mountain Smokehouse, but they wanted to push a simple message: good food, good beer. It was with this motto that they would work to bring the people of North Conway and New Hampshire top-shelf quality brews and outstanding food.

This 174-seat brew pub is packed with people no matter the season. It does not take reservations, but it is worth the wait. The overall atmosphere is inviting and filled with natural light from the large windows that line the wall. It's a best-of-both-worlds scenario for all beer drinkers. Whether you enjoy the many offerings from Moat Mountain or a Coors Light, you are in luck when you patronize this establishment. The crew at Moat Mountain prides itself on being able to offer variety to its customers. Moat Mountain understands that not all beer drinkers who walk through the door are going to be looking to have one of its original brews. However, members of the waitstaff encourage and educate when they can to offer non-craft drinkers alternatives if they want them.

Moat Mountain Smokehouse & Brewery prides itself on its high-quality food created by executive chef Scott Ross. Ross has been with Moat since 2003 and was named executive chef in 2007. He is constantly creating new and exciting things for people to try at the restaurant and continues to impress those in the community with his dishes.

The menu is filled with delicious smokehouse favorites like the Texas-style brisket or the half chicken. We recommend you try the pulled pork and change up your bread to the cinnamon raisin. You won't be disappointed. Locals flock to the restaurant to try everything from the wood-grilled pizzas or to take part in a beer dinner hosted by Chef Ross. The team is always looking to up the game in the culinary realm at Moat Mountain Smokehouse & Brewery.

A fresh pallet of Moat Mountain Iron Mike cans being delivered. *Photo courtesy of Bill Lee.*

Members of the craft beer community know that each brewery likes to have a calling card—a single defining element that helps it stand out from the rest. At Moat Mountain Smokehouse & Brewery, there are a few defining traits that set the brewpub aside from the rest. For quite some time, Moat was defined by having one of the largest cans on the market. Coming in at a daunting twenty-four ounces, the styles that were featured in this size were Iron Mike Pale Ale (a 5.6 percent ABV American pale ale brewed with three types of hops, including Cascade) and Bone Shaker Brown Ale (a 5.5 percent ABV English-style brown ale that has a rich malt body). These were Moat Mountain's calling cards in the craft beer scene. Those large cans captured the attention of the beer community and demonstrated that high-quality brews can be served in large quantities and stay consistent from the first sip to the last.

Overall, Moat Mountain brews a wide variety of beers, including Moat Czech Pilsner (a 4.9 percent ABV European-style pilsner with a medium hop bitterness and a clean floral finish) and Moat Violet B's Blueberry (a 4.5 percent American-style ale, clean and crisp with a gentle fruit finish and a medium blueberry nose). The quality of the beer is what drives Moat Mountain forward and inspires it to have its brewers try new styles that will captivate the beer scene in New Hampshire.

Head brewer and longtime Moat Mountain employee Scottie Simoneau and his assistant brewer, Matt Moore, redefine hard work in the brew house. Scottie is following in the footsteps of the original brewer at Moat Mountain, Will Gilson, who helped bring Moat Mountain to the forefront of the New Hampshire beer scene. Scottie came on in 2009, taking the opportunity and running with it. Brewing nonstop since he came on, he is continually working to hone and shape his style of brewing. With Moat Mountain gaining popularity among craft beer drinkers, its expansion plans include renovating a historic property in Intervale, New Hampshire, this year to house a new brewery with an annual capacity of over eight thousand barrels.

When we visited Moat Mountain, we were welcomed by Bill Lee, consigliere/digital sensei for Moat Mountain Smokehouse & Brewery. We were lucky enough to see everything with Bill, from the brewery's original seven-barrel system to the new facility it had renovated and was still working to finalize at the time. When we arrived at the new location, Matt Moore was brewing on the system, and everything was up and running, producing the Moat Mountain beers we have grown to love.

Moat's expansion is a testament to its growing popularity within the New Hampshire beer community. When asked about the expansion and

Moat Mountain brew house. *Photo courtesy of Bill Lee.*

Tanks on the lawn at Moat Mountain. *Photo courtesy of Bill Lee.*

other long-term plans for Moat, Lee told us that "this is the first and only expansion for us…we are comfortable with our size and how we brew beer here at Moat." This stems back to the overall theme of "great food, great beer." Keeping the beer as fresh and new as possible is the brewery's mission, and brewing on this new scale is perfectly fine with the people at Moat.

The facility itself is a gorgeous renovated old barn nestled away in the New Hampshire countryside. Sharing its property with a custom boot manufacturing facility, Peter Limmer and Sons, this new facility will allow Moat Mountain to grow to the size it wants to be. We recommend you stop in and say "Hi" to Pete and his crew and check out their amazing custom boots. It's an experience that you will not soon forget.

Bill Lee and the crew at Moat Mountain Smokehouse & Brewery sat down with us to discuss what really sets Moat aside from the rest. After an afternoon of drinking and carrying on, we settled on one theme in particular—caring. Everyone who is part of the Moat Mountain team genuinely cares about the other members and the team's goals. The comforting, inviting atmosphere at Moat Mountain is not created by a unique bar set-up or a piece of property but by the people who inhabit the community and work there everyday. The craft beer scene in New Hampshire is growing by leaps and bounds each year, and the folks at Moat Mountain are excited about it. Seeing a vast expansion in the Granite State bodes an exciting future. Being a seasoned vet in the craft beer game, Moat Mountain has established itself in the industry as a leader and will continue to do so moving into the future. Don't miss out on the best damn barbecue in the state of New Hampshire and pay Moat Mountain Smokehouse & Brewery a visit the next time you are in the mountains.

# 14
# WHITE BIRCH BREWING

## 1339 HOOKSETT ROAD, HOOKSETT
## (603) 206-5260 | WWW.WHITEBIRCBREWING.COM |
## FOUNDED 2009

In 1991, the Portsmouth Brewery started New Hampshire's first craft beer uprising. Following it were ten breweries opening over the next nine years. After Moat Mountain opened in 2000, there was silence. In 2009, Bill Herlicka introduced New Hampshire's next brewery, White Birch, which started the second and most powerful upspring on the craft beer scene.

Bill and his wife, Ellen, started the company in June 2009. As jobs started to disappear, they started to think about what they wanted to do for the next twenty years. Bill had been passionate about home-brewing since 1994. As of 2009, the state didn't have craft beer specialty stores. Most of the stores were stuck in the eighteen-pack macro-beer mentality. In order to get more craft beer on the shelves in beer stores, Bill went to work on his first beer, Belgian Pale Ale. "Belgian yeast brings great flavors and nuances to beers. You can sit down on the porch with a burger, a fish dish, and share it with friends," Bill said. When Bill would travel north to Portland, Maine, he would always seek out Allagash White, which was an inspiration to him. After two and a half years of being a brewery, White Birch opened a store to sell its beer on site. There was no sign on the building for a year, so if you wanted to find it, you had to search. The original sign was so small it is now hanging inside the current store.

White Birch is located in the town of Hooksett, New Hampshire, which is easy to get to from any direction. The brewery opened with three flagship beers: Belgian-style Pale Ale, Hop Session Ale and Hooksett Ale. Outside the flagship beers, White Birch has an extensive catalogue of labels ranging

White Birch Brewing pint. *Photo courtesy of White Birch Brewing.*

from seasonal selections, brewer's reserve, apprentice beers (more on these later) and small-batch beers only pouring at the brewery. Bill decided to streamline White Birch's portfolio so it would be easy to explain what beers were available. You will always find the flagship beers on the shelves, and depending on the season, you will find two to three more beers. For example, in the summer you can enjoy the Berliner Weisse, a 5.5 percent German-style sour wheat ale, and the Hop to Wit, a 5.3 percent Belgian-style wheat ale brewed with pink peppercorns and grapefruit.

Brewing many different styles of beer gets people excited and wanting to know what Bill will make next: "Our fans and early adopters are always asking, 'What's new'?" As a nod to the locals and fans, Bill created a small-batch label, selling growlers at the brewery. Examples of small batches include Lemon Pepper Kolsch and Bavarian Wheat, as well as beers that have the same base recipe but with a minor tweak, allowing you to taste the characteristics that different ingredients can bring to the same beer. Any of these experiments may eventually become a bottle on the shelves in stores. White Birch beer is currently available in fifteen states in twenty-two-ounce bottles and on draft and in growlers at the brewery.

## APPRENTICE PROGRAM

White Birch is well known for its Apprentice Series. Bill received constant e-mails from aspiring brewers offering help. Bill knew the only way to become a great brewer was to learn by doing. In 2009, the same year White Birch opened, the Apprentice Program began. White Birch's first apprentice was Matt McComish. His first task was a messy one. In the brew house there were fermenters that once held Cherry Quad. These fermenters had yeast, cherries and cherry pits caked all over the inside. What better job for Matt than to clean them? Much to everyone's surprise, Matt cleaned them and, covered head to toe in filth, asked, "What are we doing next week?" Although the apprentices are not paid, Bill created an incentive for them. At the end of his or her apprenticeship, each apprentice gets to brew a beer. This beer is bottled and available at the brewery for anyone to purchase. This "graduation" commences with a big party at the brewery at which the beer is finally released. In Matt's case, he brewed and released a beer called Aloha, a Belgian wit with fruit notes and a hint of spice. White Birch's first female apprentice was Beth Eisenberg. Her graduation beer was a Scotch ale called Broustaris, which is a Scottish term for the women brewers of the Middle Ages.

As of 2013, seventeen people have gone through the program, bringing a lot of fun energy to the brewery as well as new and interesting beers for the locals to taste. The apprentices have gone on to grow in the beer industry. Some have even started breweries in New York, Vermont and Tennessee. Most recently, John Cataldo, now part of the quality team at Boston's Harpoon Brewery, released the forty-ninth beer of Harpoon's One-Hundred-Barrel Series, Brown IPA. White Birch chronicles all of its apprentice beers on its website, complete with descriptions and words from the apprentices themselves. For someone who opened a brewery to fulfill his own dreams, starting the Apprentice Program in the same year shows a sign of passion. Bill is letting these brewers enjoy the same ride he is on.

# THE BEER LOVER'S FESTIVAL

Bill wanted to create a festival that had everything you love about a festival (great beer and food) and take out everything you hate about a festival (drink tickets and expensive food). It is on these principles that Bill created the annual Southern New Hampshire Brewers Festival. This festival is one of the most talked about in the state. The festival is a way to celebrate what White Birch does every year and share it with other brewers. The price of the ticket includes everything: parking, water, beer and food. All of the food is cooked on site. Mouth-watering examples include a pig roast, cupcakes made with beer and cotton candy made with beer and bacon. Don't worry, there are vegetarian options available. There is also a cigar tent from the cigar shop Twins Smoke Shop, an institution in New Hampshire. This is truly a beer fest of epic proportions, loved by beer fans and brewers.

We say Bill Herlicka is a brewer for the people. He allows others to take a journey into the world of brewing as well as puts on a festival that outdoes many other festivals of its kind. The team at White Birch can be seen at many other events around New England pouring its new beers and the beers that started the brewery.

# 15
# THE PRODIGAL BREWERY

## 684 TOWN HOUSE ROAD, EFFINGHAM
## (603) 539-2210 | WWW.THEPRODIGALBREWERY.COM |
## FOUNDED 2009

In the early 1990s, Paul Davis was a bartender and a home-brewer. Most of the beers he was brewing were beers that were not readily available, such as German ales or lagers. In 1995, he went out to UC–Davis to study with Dr. Michael Lewis and Dr. Ashton Lewis. After returning from the program, Richard Young took him under his wing at the now defunct Castle Springs Brewery. He showed him how important the water source is in brewing beer. Paul then became the assistant brewer at Lucknow in Moultonborough, New Hampshire, also now out of business. From there, he went to Trout Brook/Thomas Hooker Brewing in Hartford, Connecticut. After years of working there, Paul wanted to open his own brewery. In 2009, he began to make his dream a reality.

Effingham is the crossroad of New England, and Paul and his wife picked the spot due to its wide array of agricultural resources. They have a family farm with crops planted specifically for the brewery. They have raspberries, blueberries, rye and buckwheat, as well as an organic hops certification. His wife is a beekeeper, and her bees provide a source of honey for some of his beers. One of Paul's goals is to brew an estate-only beer—a beer with all ingredients harvested from the brewery farm. Paul is bringing the brewing tradition back to the farm. "Wine has done a wonderful job showcasing how you can make wine on the vineyard. Brewing has lost its way," Paul said. "Beer comes from agricultural processes. We are in an agricultural business. Maybe people will understand it is important to keep and preserve these farms because someone has to grow the malt, hops, barley." One of Paul's flagship beers is the Effingham Burgerbrau, a Munich helles. This beer, along with his other beers, is what he likes to drink and had a hard time finding when he was a home-brewer.

In 2012, Prodigal was looking to expand, so Paul reached out to his fans for support. He utilized the website Kickstarter to raise funds for more equipment. "We had been slowly picking up the dream equipment together. We had very specific needs to produce the authentic beers we wanted to make, and we found this equipment in British Columbia," Paul explained. The shipping from Vancouver to Effingham was expensive. Paul had a specific number in mind to make it work: $6,324. "Our ten-hectoliter horizontal-lagering tanks hold over twenty-five barrels of beer, which is about 6,324 pints. If we had a dollar for every potential pint, we'd be well along the path to fill those tanks," he said. Prodigal reached its goal, and Paul has the names of his supporters in his brewery in the form of paper pint glasses. He even brought the list of names to the American Craft Beer Festival in Boston as a show of thanks. The new brewing system has been working since May 2013.

Finding beer from Prodigal is currently a challenge, but the reward is worth the search. Paul can be seen at various festivals in New England, usually with his family. He designed his brewery as a family business and likes family-friendly events. You can currently find Prodigal's beers at a few beer stores in Carroll County. Sometimes, a tap will show up in a bar on the seacoast. After legislation (HB1172) was passed, breweries can now sell beer at farmers' markets. "It's a great way of selling beer to our neighbors," Paul explained. Paul also enjoys putting his beer in casks, which he calls "the fine art of handling beer." In 2014, the Coat of Arms Pub in Portsmouth featured casks from Prodigal one day during Portsmouth Beer Week. One of his most interesting beers is the Curse of the RyeWolf Roggenbier, which features Jason Sanderson on the label. Jason is a writer and family friend and blessed the brewery. He has a past life as the Wolfman in professional wrestling.

Whenever you have the chance to see Paul and his family at a festival or farmers' market you are in for a treat. His beers are some of the most unique in the state. Prodigal Brewery beers should be more available in the near future so everyone can get their hands on great German-style ales and lagers from the crossroads of New England—Effingham, New Hampshire.

# 16
# THROWBACK BREWERY

## 121 LAFAYETTE ROAD, NORTH HAMPTON
## (603) 379-2317 | WWW.THROWBACKBREWERY.COM |
## FOUNDED 2010

The brewing scene was quiet in the seacoast for much of the early 2000s. You could consider this the calm before the storm for New Hampshire craft beer. According to New Hampshire law, a nanobrewery is a brewery that produces fewer than two thousand barrels of beer annually. It only costs $240 to obtain a nanobrewery license. In July 2011, the seacoast area of New Hampshire was introduced to its first nanobrewery. Nicole Carrier and Annette Lee started Throwback Brewery in North Hampton as a way to combine a passion for home-brewing and support local agriculture. Their goal was and still is to make good beer with ingredients found within two hundred miles of the brewery. They would like to source 100 percent of their ingredients locally, but the cost of doing so is high. All of Throwback's wheat comes from New Hampshire, and 60 to 70 percent of its barley comes from Massachusetts and eastern New York. A lot of its hops come from Westfield, Maine's Aroostook Hops. The brewery also works with local farmers for a lot of the adjuncts. For example, ingredients like jalapeños for the Spicy Bohemian beer come from New Roots Farm. (We describe that beer as liquid nachos in the best way.)

Throwback's malted barley comes from Valley Malt in Hadley, Massachusetts. In 2010, Nicole's cousin Andrea Stanley started Valley Malt with her husband, Christian, as a way to produce barley for brewers to use in their brewing processes. Currently, Valley Malt operates on a total of seventy acres, producing four tons of malted barley in a weekend. Andrea and Christian plan to continue to grow and produce more. Valley Malt is

Annette Lee, co-owner of Throwback Brewery. *Photo courtesy of Throwback Brewery.*

a huge buzzword that you will hear from many breweries in New England and beyond. Throwback isn't the only company to use malt from Valley Malt. As far south as Rehoboth Beach, Delaware (Dogfish Head Brewery); as far west as Burdett, New York (Finger Lakes Distilling); and as far North as Freeport, Maine (Maine Beer Company), Valley Malt has a list of twenty-eight breweries and five distilleries using its malt. Just like its business, the list of breweries that use and support Valley Malt is growing fast.

No matter where you are in New England, any craft beer geek will mention Throwback as one of the greats. Throwback opened its three-barrel system with tremendous support from the community. Usually with anything new, the initial pandemonium will eventually die down, but not with Throwback. The business park where Throwback currently resides is packed every week with thirsty tourists and fans, and you will find its beers at most bars on the seacoast. Their flagship beers include Hog Happy Hefeweizen, Dippity Do American Brown Ale, Campfire Smoked Porter, Maple Wheat Porter, Love Me Long Time Pilsener and Hopstruck IPA. It seems every brewery nowadays has a rare beer that's worth camping out for. There is no doubt that the Fat Alberta Chocolate Peanut Butter Stout is the beer worth waiting for at Throwback. Once a year, the beer is released at the brewery with a

Nicole Carrier, co-owner of Throwback Brewery offers up a sample. *Photo courtesy of Throwback Brewery.*

party. For those in to casks and firkins, you can always find a cask or two from Throwback at the Coat of Arms in Portsmouth.

Throwback also has a great club for stout lovers, the Unafraid of the Dark program. Each stout showcases an ingredient from a local farm. Examples range from Chocolate Ginger Stout, Fennel Flower Stout, Chai Porter using White Heron tea, Squash Porter from Brookford Farms, New Roots Bacon Porter, Caramel Apple Milk Stout, Chipotle Porter, Coffee Milk Stout using Red Rover Coffee, Chocolate Mint Stout, Chocolate Beet Stout, Chaga Porter and Pumpkin Chai. Thirsty yet?

With the passing of New Hampshire bill HB1172, breweries can now sell beer at farmers' markets. This aligns perfectly with Throwback's model. Now you can purchase its beer, made with ingredients from local farms, and purchase other goods from those farms all in the same place. The future is surely all about growth. In 2012, Throwback purchased the twelve-acre Hobbs Farm at auction. The farm is across the street from Throwback's current location. This will upgrade the brewery's brewing system to fifteen barrels. The farm came complete with Jericho, a donkey for which the Double IPA Donkey-Hote, is named. Throwback Brewery currently has a great tasting room, where you can stop in for some samples and purchase bottles, growlers and other merchandise. Nicole and Annette are always coming up with new recipes and releasing them to the thirsty beer fans of the world.

# 17
# EARTH EAGLE BREWINGS

## 165 HIGH STREET, PORTSMOUTH
## (603) 817-2773 | WWW.EARTHEAGLEBREWINGS.COM |
## FOUNDED 2012

B utch Heilshorn and Alex McDonald are the mad scientist brewers of
Earth Eagle Brewings in Portsmouth, New Hampshire. They started
as home-brewers brewing a clone of Dogfish Head's World Wide Stout and
are now operating one of the most popular breweries in the state. What sets
Earth Eagle apart from other breweries is its take on traditional beer recipes.
Alex and Butch reintroduced the gruit style of beer to the state, a medieval
style of beer brewed until the sixteenth century that is brewed with herbs in
place of hops. Butch's wife, an herbalist, had many herbs at hand for Butch
and Alex to try as ingredients in their beers. The idea came from Stephen
Buhner's book *Sacred and Herbal Healing Beers: The Secrets of Ancient Fermentation*.

Before Earth Eagle opened, Alex opened a home-brew supply shop with
his wife (Butch's sister), Gretchen, to fill a void on the seacoast. At the time,
Alex and Butch had to drive hours to get supplies for their home-brews.
After years of research, they settled on a building in downtown Portsmouth.
A year after opening A&G Homebrew Supply, they began to renovate half
of the shop's space for Earth Eagle Brewings. Despite wanting to start out
with a ten-gallon brewing system, Butch and Alex decided on a one-barrel
brewing system after receiving feedback from other brewers to start bigger.

Earth Eagle introduced something to the craft beer community that
hadn't been tried at the time—taking risks with ingredients more suited for
food than drink—and it worked. A lot of the beers brewed here haven't been
done before and are as approachable as any other beer in the country. Sitting
at the bar listening to Alex, Butch or any one of their expert beertenders

talk about the ingredients in a particular beer is a fascinating experience. Ingredients that you think would turn someone away, like a hog's head, a rose-hip or lilac beer, actually intrigues even the newest to craft beer. "A lot of breweries get trapped in the fact that they can't brew something obscure and different because they are brewing in such large quantity," Alex says. "People are dying to get into different territories to try different tastes. Gruits seem to be a gateway beer for a lot of people who think they don't like beer. Initially, they are scared, but once they taste it, they get it." When it comes to the gruits, it's all about what is available. Earth Eagle looks to Jenna Roselle, a professional forager who goes out in the woods and gets herbs for the brewers and many local restaurants. Whatever is brought back is used in its next creation.

The best part about the popularity of Earth Eagle, besides its size, is how many beers it has. In a week, you will see a tap list of six beers, and the following week you will see a different list. Brewing in small batches means beers will run out quickly, leaving fans drooling for the next beer to be tapped. The brewery doesn't just brew gruits. You will find anything from hoppy to Belgian to sour to stout in the rotation. The New England Gangsta is a beer loaded with citra, amarillo and cascade hops, along with West Coast ale yeast giving off fruity esters. Their Shepherd's Crook, a wheat pale ale with 50 percent wheat malt, is loaded with all New Zealand hops (green bullet, motueka, nelson savant) giving off a pineapple–white grape finish. We wouldn't be doing this book justice without mentioning Porter Cochon, a porter brewed with an actual pig's head in the boil of the beer. Many did not believe, including vegetarians, but be warned: it is true. It is experiments like this that make locals and beer fans come running to Earth Eagle to see what it will have next. Alex and Butch push each other's boundaries to put forth beer that is flavorful and has a story behind it.

"Throwback made it easy for a lot of smaller breweries by being the first nano to open on the seacoast. The big question is are you into it for the beer or the money? The people who are really into the beer will be the ones to last," Butch said.

In 2013, Strawbery Banke held the exhibit "Tapping Portsmouth," which highlighted the rich brewing history of Portsmouth. To celebrate the opening, the museum held an event to highlight old recipes. Earth Eagle was one of the breweries called on to celebrate. Alex and Butch brewed a beer called Scorbutus, a colonial ale brewed with molasses, parsnips and oats. The beer was served in the William Pit Tavern, one of the oldest taverns in Portsmouth. The likes of George Washington and John Hancock once drank there. "It's goosebump city," Butch said.

On the home-brewing side of the business, Alex and Gretchen have frequent Meet the Brewer nights where they bring in a respected brewer from the area to talk beer with fans and aspiring brewers. They also teach home-brewing classes that let you enter the world of making your own beer. If you have the equipment but are looking for a recipe, you can ask them to create one for you. A&G is also home to the Seacoast Homebrew Club's monthly meetings. If you are a home-brewer, your beer could be brewed at Earth Eagle if you are lucky. Once a year, the club holds a competition in which the best home-brew voted on by the members is brewed at the brewery.

The taproom of Earth Eagle was built by Alex and Butch and has a nice speakeasy feel to it. Lining the walls are old hiking trail and ski slope signs, and in nice weather, the garage door opens up, letting a nice breeze inside. If you are lucky enough, you may see Alex and Butch brewing in the brew house as you are having one of their beers in the taproom. In early 2014, Earth Eagle received the license to cook food and serve larger-sized beers. Now you can get half pints, pints and, if you were one of the lucky few who signed up, twenty-ounce chalices of beer. The food features meat and cheeses from the acclaimed Black Trumpet restaurant of Portsmouth, as well as soups and stews that really highlight the beers made mere steps away from where you're eating the food. If you haven't been to Earth Eagle yet, there is no bad time to go. You are bound to find something new each and every time you visit.

18

# 603 BREWERY

## 12 LIBERTY DRIVE #7, LONDONDERRY (603) 630-7745 | WWW.603BREWERY.COM | FOUNDED 2012

The 603 Brewery located in Londonderry, New Hampshire, is one of the younger breweries in the New Hampshire beer market. It was established in 2012 by a trio of beer lovers whose friendship stems back to their college days: Geoff and Tamsin Hewes and Dan Leonard. Their love for beer has brought them to the main stage in the New Hampshire beer scene. They have shown the New Hampshire community what hard work is all about.

Dan started his brewing career back in college almost fifteen years ago as a home-brewer. Honing his skills and creating quality, replicable brews was important to him as a home-brewer. Testing his brews on family and friends for years, Dan always knew in the back of his head that this was something he could do professionally.

When the idea to start a brewery came to the forefront, Geoff, Tamsin and Dan were all hands on deck to make it happen. The three of them started their careers on the engineering front, but when those careers became monotonous and dry, the desire for something bigger arose.

This group has truly redefined the phrase "lean and mean." With a heavy focus on maximizing the potential output of every brew, the 603 crew is hungry and looking to make a big impact in the ever-expanding landscape of New Hampshire brewing. The trio's skillset focuses heavily on their hard work and dedication to their brand. Geoff, being the production manager of the group, is in charge of streamlining operations throughout the brewery. Dan, a water quality specialist, brings his expertise right to the foundation of the beer, working to make every drop perfect. Lastly, Tamsin's love of marketing and retail has sculpted the 603 brand into what promises to be a staple for years to come.

Moving into a proper brewing space in 2012 was a huge step forward for this blossoming brewery. Expanding its space from a nanobrewery to a larger-scale microbrewery has given it the ability to expand its bottling efforts and bring more products to the restaurant scene via kegs. Although the facility is small, Geoff, Tamsin and Dan have worked to make their brewery exude a homey feel. The little details truly shine through as soon as you walk through the door. The 603 team has worked to make its patrons feel welcome from the moment they enter the space. From the unfinished wooden shelving to the state-of-the-art brewing equipment, this little brewery has worked to capture what it means to brew in New Hampshire. A healthy combination of simple and complex has transformed this old storage unit into a location where beer can be produced, bottled and enjoyed by the general public.

Its lineup of beers include Winni Ale, Amber Ale, White Peaks White IPA, 18 Mile Ale, Rye Pale Ale, 9th State Red IPA and Cogway IPA. With a wide and powerful variety of beers, 603 Brewing Company is looking to take the New Hampshire brewing scene by storm. Look for it to grow within the New Hampshire brewing community and continue to contribute to this exciting time in beer history.

# 19

# HENNIKER BREWING COMPANY

## 129 CENTERVALE ROAD, HENNIKER
## (603) 428-3579 | WWW.HENNIKERBREWING.COM |
## FOUNDED 2011

Former state senator David Currier opened Henniker Brewing Company with James Moriarty as the head brewer in 2012. The brewery is located in—you guessed it—Henniker, New Hampshire. The brewery is proof that you can open and operate a brewery in a nontourist area successfully. In 2013, Chris Shea stepped in as head brewer, bringing with him a solid brewing résumé.

One of Chris Shea's influences is Dan Paquette of Pretty Things Beer and Ale Project. "I like his attitude toward making beer the kind of community they are trying to create at Pretty Things. It elevates beer to the level of art in a very unique way," Chris said. Chris started home-brewing the same year Paquette opened his brewery in 2009. Chris moved to St. Louis, where he got a job shoveling mash at Morgan Street Brewery for two years under the direction of Marc Gottfried. He then gave tours at Schlafly Bottleworks while working the bottling line at Schlafly Taproom. Chris moved back east, where he worked for White Birch Brewing Company for two years before taking over the fifteen-barrel system at Henniker in mid-2013.

What makes Chris one of the more unique brewers in the state is his affinity for stouts and porters made before the 1900s. When he started drinking craft beer, he wanted to know the difference between porters and stouts. No one could give him a straight answer; some to this day can't tell the difference. Dan Paquette lent Chris Ron Pattinson's book *Porter!*, which traces the history of the style from the 1700s to World War II. He found his

Henniker Brewing Company pint glasses. *Photo courtesy of Henniker Brewing Company.*

Thirsty crowd at Henniker Brewing Company. *Photo courtesy of Henniker Brewing Company.*

answer. Porters are made with pale, brown and black malt, and stouts are made with pale, brown and burned black malt. Chris took this knowledge to develop one of Henniker's flagships and bestselling beers, the Working Man's Porter. The three other flagships include Hopslinger IPA, Amber Apparition and Whipple's Wheat. What makes Whipple's Wheat stand out is Chris's take on the style. This dry-hopped wheat ale is citrusy and flavorful with a little bitterness and a big wheat finish. Henniker's winter seasonal, The Roast, is a stout with fifteen pounds of coffee from White Mountain Coffee Company. Their spring seasonal is D.H. Double IPA. The best part about the double IPA is the recipe will be different each year, allowing Chris to highlight new experimental strains of hops. You can visit the brewery any day of the week to fill up a growler of one of its flagships, and if you're lucky, there might be a special small batch on tap like the Whipple's Wheat with pressed apples.

Henniker Brewing Company is distributed in twenty-two-ounce bottles all over the state: Bellavance Beverage in southeastern New Hampshire, Clarke Distributors in the southwest and Great State Distribution in the north. The small team at the brewery is running all over the state quenching the thirst of craft beer fans.

# So You Want to Be a Brewer, Eh?

In July 2013, Chris penned a guest post on the Dig Boston blog in response to the growing fascination of craft beer brewing. A lot of you who are reading this book are craft beer enthusiasts and may see the job of running a brewery as all fun and games. Chris tried to set the story straight with his column "So You Want to Be a Brewer, Eh?" Chris explains that brewing is not always the glorified dream job of standing behind a table at beer fests pouring beer. It is long, hard work with twelve-hour shifts: "Brewing work comes to no man! Another reason married men rarely become brewers. You gotta be open to work anywhere in the country." He ends the post with "We're janitors who get free beer. It's not all that bad, but it's certainly not cool or glamorous. Chances are, if you were supposed to be a brewer, you'd probably already be one by that point." It is a must read for anyone looking to see what brewing is like through the eyes of a brewer.

20

# GREAT RHYTHM BREWING COMPANY

PO BOX 1624, PORTSMOUTH
(603) 300-8588 | WWW.GREATRHYTHMBREWING.COM |
FOUNDED 2012

The story of Great Rhythm Brewing Company reveals the loving attitude of founders Scott and Kristen Thornton. They noticed that wherever they were having a good time with friends and family, there was good craft beer close by. With plenty of great beer to be had from coast to coast, they wanted to add to the craft beer scene in Portsmouth, New Hampshire.

Scott worked for Mercury Brewing Company out of Ipswich, Massachusetts. Mercury Brewing Company is home to many breweries, in fact. This is due in part to contract brewing. Contract brewing is when a bigger company, like Mercury, rents its equipment and space to other breweries that do not have physical locations. Breweries who brew out of Mercury's facility include Cambridge Brewing Company, Notch and Slumbrew, among others. During his time working here, Scott brewed a lot of beer on a commercial scale while passionately home-brewing in hopes of one day opening a brewery. He approached Mercury about contract brewing there to be able to get Great Rhythm beer into the hands of his and Kristen's hometown, Portsmouth, where they plan to have an actual facility based in the future. This was a great way to get started on a large scale and get the beer out to the community. The relationship with Mercury gives Great Rhythm a lot of hands-on control with the beer. It is a good balance between brewing and allowing for promoting at events. Scott and Kristen are hoping the positive response to Resonation Pale Ale will help them afford a place in Portsmouth.

Great Rhythm Brewing logo. *Photo courtesy of Great Rythym Brewing Company.*

"There are a lot of the un-fun aspects of starting a brewery. One of those is writing a business plan. As far as getting the beer out there, one thing we did for ourselves was write down 'living life to the fullest with great friends, great music and great craft beer,'" Scott said. He always jotted on a notebook to keep focused. "It's not easy to be a small craft brewer, and it is harder to get your beer out there to people. You need inspiration."

Great Rhythm's flagship Resonation Pale Ale is derived from a trip to Colorado and seeing Fat Tire in all the bars, music venues and festivals. "That beer represents a feeling of having good times with friends. It tastes different every time you drink it because you are drinking it in a different place and time that enhances the overall beer drinking experience," Kristen said. Based on these experiences, they created Resonation Pale Ale, a more hop-forward pale ale that lets your senses bring you back to a good place. "We really like hop aroma in beer," Scott said. "There are great IPAs out there that are bitter but can't be enjoyed all day at festivals with your friends." Great Rhythm's 5.2 percent ABV pale ale is light and refreshing and can be found year round. You can't miss Resonation on the shelf because of the great label art created by two local artists.

Although Great Rhythm currently has no location in New Hampshire, it is on many tap handles across the seacoast. The brewing community is also very supportive of the brewery. During the fourth annual Portsmouth Beer Week, Tyler Jones of the Portsmouth Brewery invited Scott and Kristen to collaborate on a beer. "It was great to play around with different types of malts and grains that we don't typically use in our system in Ipswich," Scott said. They ended up brewing a beer called Total Eclipse of the Stout. Scott always wanted to brew a stout and enjoyed experimenting with different ingredients. They used midnight wheat malt, which led to a smooth, balanced stout that had a taste of chocolate and was paired nicely with hazelnut brittle. Raise a glass to a brewery invested in making sure your experience with their beer is always a good time.

# SPOTLIGHT

## *Portsmouth Beer Week*

Started in 2009 by the group of beer enthusiasts at 2Beerguys.com, Portsmouth Beer Week is indeed the greatest week in craft beer on the seacoast. Every night during the week, there are multiple beer events going on. From special beer releases to beer fests to dinners and tastings, there is something for everyone. Portsmouth Beer Week actually runs for ten days, allowing beer fans to enjoy two weekends of beer events. The theme of camaraderie that all of the local breweries have is multiplied during the week. You will see brewers showing up to events involving other breweries to show support and to drink their beers. For some, Portsmouth Beer Week is a good time to launch a brewery. In 2014, Stoneface Brewing Company of Newington, New Hampshire, released its beer for the first time at the Seacoast Winter Brew Fest, one of the beer week's main events, as well as a launch event at the Coat of Arms.

# 21

# THE FUTURE OF NEW HAMPSHIRE BEER

The future of craft beer in New Hampshire is strong, my thirsty friends. With new breweries popping up all over the country, the Granite State is seeing a very high increase in those taking the leap to open a production brewery and attract beer enthusiasts from around the country.

## 7ᵀᴴ SETTLEMENT/ONE LOVE BREWERY

*47 Washington Street, Dover*
*(603) 373-1001 | www.7thsettlement.com | www.onelovebrewery.com*
*Founded 2013*

Dover, New Hampshire, was once home to the Barley Pub, a staple in the craft beer industry of the seacoast. This beer bar was one of those places where brewers would meet for a pint after work and stay until the bands finished playing. Rare beers would show up on tap like Paul Davis's Prodigal Brewery beers because Barley Pub was a beer lover's bar. Before its closing, a new brewery opened up down the street. In fact, two breweries under the same roof opened. One Love Brewery and 7ᵗʰ Settlement are located in the Cocheco Falls Millworks in downtown Dover.

Michael Snyder is the brewer in charge of One Love Brewery, and Josh Henry and Nate Sephton brew at 7ᵗʰ Settlement. The idea is to split a seven-barrel brewery under the same roof and, with the help of a kitchen that is focused on sustainability, provide a unique pub experience. Most of the food served in the completely restored pub space is sourced locally. Brewer Michael Snyder has a large-brewing background. He spent some time at Redhook Ale Brewery in Portsmouth and Hofbrauhaus Brewery and Biergarten at Station Casino and 75th Street Brewery in Kansas City, Missouri. The custom-built brew house contains both breweries, known as New England's first "co-op brewery." You will find beers on draft from both breweries as well as guest taps for other local breweries. Some of their flagship beers include One Love's UntzUntzUntz Kolsch and 7th Settlement's 1896 Cocheco Winter Wheat.

# Blue Lobster Brewing Company

*845 Lafayette Road, Hampton*
*(603) 601-6062 | www.bluelobsterbrew.com | Founded 2012*

Blue Lobster Brewing Company is one of the newest breweries to pop up in the seacoast region of New Hampshire. This nanobrewery has developed quite a bit since its launch in 2012. Founded by longtime home-brewer Michael Benoit and his wife, Roberta, it has focused on quite an array of brews in its short time on the scene. With its focus being on diversity, the Blue Lobster crew is looking to share a wide variety of beers with the general public. Brewing such beers as their Gold Claw Pale Ale to Black Claw Stout, this group wants to bring to the seacoast a fresh take on some old favorites.

Blue Lobster's location is ideal for a quick stop on the weekend to enjoy one of the brews on tap in its cozy, yet modern tasting room. High-top tables line the room in this small nanobrewery that can be visited Wednesday through Sunday most weeks. Be sure to check the brewery's hours online to ensure you are able to get a taste or pick up a bottle or two at the facility. Located just twenty minutes outside the coastal beer town of Portsmouth and minutes from Hampton Beach, we recommend you stop in and pay Blue Lobster Brewing a visit the next time you are in the area and looking for a beer. With a few changes in its processes, Blue Lobster is still looking to grow in this vast beer market. Blue Lobster Brewing aims to make its mark in the beer scene as the market continues to evolve in New Hampshire. Keep an eye out for the brewery and what it has in store for the future.

# BORDER BREW SUPPLY

*10 Lawrence Road, Salem*
*(603) 216-9134 | www.borderbrewsupply.com | Founded 2013*

Any home-brewer knows that practice makes perfect. Well, that's just the excuse we tell ourselves to brew more beer. Whether you are a rookie on the home-brewing scene or an expert, we recommend that you stop in and pay Border Brew Supply a visit. Located just off Interstate 93 in Salem, New Hampshire, Border Brew Supply is the place to be whether you are home-brewing beer or wine. The brewing scene in New Hampshire is expanding rapidly, and with rapid expansion comes the need for supplies and knowledge. Border Brew Supply has just that.

Whether you are stopping in to pick up tools, supplies or ingredients, the crew at Border Brew Supply will give you the guidance and knowledge you need to brew a stellar batch of beer (or wine). With a strong focus on bettering our communities, Border Brew Supply wants you to enjoy yourself with a hobby such as home-brewing. The store is looking to improve the health of our global community through the purchase of fair-trade products. Stop in soon to pay a visit and plan your next home-brewing session! Did we mention the store also has beer on tap? So you can stop in for supplies and try some of its beers too!

# CANDIA ROAD BREWING COMPANY

*840 Candia Road, Manchester*
*(603) 935-8123 | www.candiaroad.com | Founded 2012*

Established by the brothers of the Titone and Neel families in 2012, this Manchester storefront is home to a large assortment of microbrews. With a heavy focus on variety, this store was established during the rise of the craft beer movement in New Hampshire. Offering craft beer, cigars, pipe tobacco and even a full-service deli, the crew at Candia Road has established a one-stop shop for beer drinkers. At this location, you can sample and purchase the store's own brand of beer. The Nepenthe brand is brewed on site and can be sampled at such locations as Strange Brew and the Four Points Sheraton in Manchester, New Hampshire. Stop in and pay them a visit the next time you find yourself in the area!

# Canterbury Ale Works

### 305 Baptist Hill Road, Canterbury
### (603) 491-4539 | www.canterburyaleworks.com | Founded 2013

This brewery is a one-man show. Owner, operator and head brewer Steve Allman is the heart and soul of Canterbury Ale Works in Canterbury, New Hampshire, located just twenty minutes north of Concord. This one-barrel brewery can brew batches of whatever he pleases. This is a huge positive for a smaller system—it promotes variety and unique beers for the community to sample. Steve offers a variety of beers ranging from Be Hoppy! IPA to his Old Darn Bard British brown ale. Offering his beers in both twenty-two-ounce bottles and growler pours, Steve is off to a great start brewing in the New Hampshire beer scene and looks to continue his one-man show into the coming years. Be sure to stop in and pay him a visit the next time you are near Concord.

# IncrediBREW

### 112 Daniel Webster Highway, Nashua
### (603) 891-2477 | www.incredibrew.com | Founded 1995

The future of New Hampshire craft beer could actually be in your hands. At IncrediBREW in Nashua, New Hampshire, you can learn how to make beer. IncrediBREW calls itself "Your Personal Brewery," and it means it. To start, you pick a recipe from its ever-updating list of beers. Then, you brew it at IncrediBREW's facility using its equipment and ingredients. The beer is stored for two weeks until you return to bottle it and take home. You don't need to mess up your kitchen or pots and pans. The ease behind this model can turn the curious home-brewer into an aspiring production brewer.

# SCHILLING BEER COMPANY

*18 Mill Street, Littleton*
*(603) 444-4800 | www.schillingbeer.com | Founded 2013*

The best part about taking a craft beer adventure is not knowing what to expect. When you speak with brewers and beer lovers, you will get suggestions that will change your itinerary for the better. While interviewing Rik Marley of Flying Goose, we were asked what our plans were for the day. Explaining our next stop was to go to Woodstock Inn Station & Brewery and spend the night in that area, Rik said, "Nope, cancel your motel plans and spend the night in Littleton. Go to Schilling. These guys have amazing pizza and awesome beer." If you ever have the opportunity to change your schedule on a whim and go to an unknown place, do it. Truth be told, Schilling was not even on the radar for this book. That changed when we pulled into Littleton, New Hampshire.

The town of Littleton, New Hampshire, does not scream craft beer destination. It's a nice little town with great shops and remarkably friendly people. It's well suited for hikers and skiers to come and stay after a long day on the mountains. In fact, Italian Oasis, one of the oldest brewpubs in the state, still operates in the town center and fires up the beer kettle from time to time. Just down the road from here is Schilling Beer Company. Schilling is owned by brothers Jeff, Matt and Stuart Cozzens, with John Lenzini at the helm as brewer. When you walk into the brewpub, you instantly smell the wood-fired pizza as you look out across the first floor of the eighteenth-century mill building. The tap list features the brewpub's own creations and guest taps, both local and outside the region.

Brewer John Lenzini is quite literally the mad scientist behind the brews at Schilling. He is a chemist/educator and began perfecting European styles of beer as a home-brewer in 1997. Styles we tasted were a Belgian trippel, Baltic porter, Belgian strong, Belgian pale and hefeweizen. It's important to note that this brewery opened in May 2013 in a small town thirty miles north of the closest craft brewery (Woodstock). With breweries opening faster than you can drink a beer, one can understand breweries taking risks to stand out in the crowd. Without styles like the hoppy IPAs or a simple pale ale, can Schilling pull it off? In a word, yes—undeniably, without a doubt yes. As we were tasting its beers, we had to keep asking if it had only been open for six months. Schilling is the perfect example for the future of craft beer in New

Hampshire. There is hope for breweries to open up and succeed even in remote towns, so long as the beer is great. It also helps the Cozzen brothers. Brewer John and staff are friendly to boot. Schilling Beer Company makes great beer, and we cannot wait to see more from it.

## STONEFACE BREWING COMPANY

*436 Shattuck Way, Newington*
*(603) 498-0211 | www.stonefacebrewing.com | Founded 2014*

It's been over ten years since the Old Man of the Mountain, aka the Great Stone Face, fell from his perch atop Cannon Cliffs, but one brewery in the Granite State is keeping his spirit alive. Stoneface Brewing Company was founded in 2013 by two New Hampshire natives and a New York

Stoneface Brewing logo. *Photo courtesy of Stoneface.*

transplant. The brewery has started with several hop-forward beers, including Stoneface IPA, which is dry hopped with an irresponsible amount of citra and amarillo hops.

Stoneface Brewing Company is a fifteen-barrel production brewery located just south of the historic General Sullivan Bridge at exit 4 off the Spaulding Turnpike in Newington, New Hampshire. Its beers can be found in bars and restaurants along the seacoast, and its bottles can be found in shops across the state. When you're headed for ski country or the lakes region and find yourself stuck on Route 16 northbound in rush-hour traffic on a Friday afternoon, be sure to stop for a growler fill.

# Squam Brewing

## *118 Perch Pond Road, Holderness*
## *(603) 236-9705 | www.squambrewing.com | Founded 2010*

The lakes region of New Hampshire is a breathtaking array of scenery that allows you to get away from it all. A quick trip up Interstate 93 from Manchester will have you to this location in roughly an hour. Any lover of nature should take a trip to the lakes region, and while you are there, stop in and visit Squam Brewery.

Located in Holderness, New Hampshire, Squam Brewery is right in the middle of a gorgeous landscape. Established in 2010, this small two- to three-barrel brewery, which does all its brewing out of a barn, is quite the sight to see. Doing all its brewing in a 145-gallon stout kettle that the owners retrofitted themselves allows the brewery to provide great beer to the people of New Hampshire. In order to take a tour, be sure to visit Squam's website and contact the brewery directly. You can pick up its beer in twenty-two-ounce bottles and kegs around New Hampshire.

# David Sakolsky

Since this chapter's main focus is on the breweries of the future, this is a great place to mention a stellar upcoming brewer. We found ourselves sitting down for a pint at WHYM Craft Beer bar with the one and only David Sakolsky.

May 2014 will mark five years in the brewing game for David Sakolsky. One of New Hampshire's premier brewers is just getting his feet wet in the brewing pond, but in his five-year stint, he has obtained a lifetime's worth of brewing knowledge.

David entered the brewing game as a way to subsidize his love for craft beer. A freelance advertiser at the time, he found his way into the home-brewing world and never looked back. A Vermonter when he first began brewing, David found himself trying a Dogfish Head Palo Santo over a slice of pizza. A wood-aged, American brown ale that is raw in flavor and design is what brought him into the craft world. Aside from the occasional Seven Barrel Brewery or Yuengling, he had never really drifted into the craft beer arena. It was uncharted territory, and he was looking to learn more about this blossoming portion of the beer community. After spending his fair share at Winooski Beverage, located in scenic Winooski, Vermont, he decided that it was time to create some beers of his own. This was the start of something great for David, and on an unseasonably warm day in October, he filled us in on what became his journey into the world of craft brewing.

"It's all works in progress" was how he led off the interview. A resident rock star in the brewing community, David has brewed at White Birch Brewing in Hooksett, New Hampshire; Hill Farmstead Brewery in Greensboro Bend, Vermont; and Blue Lobster Brewing Company in Hampton, New Hampshire. His focus is on consistency and creativity in his brews. After coming close to exceeding the legal limit for brewing (one hundred gallons per person per household), David went looking for a way to learn more about the world of beer. At this time in the craft beer game, there weren't as many players as there are now. He was in search of a location where he could actually learn about brewing hands on as opposed to working on a bottling line somewhere. This took him to White Birch Brewing in the Granite State. In time, David's apprenticeship at White Birch under Bill Herlicka helped him develop his budding skillset. He did his fair share of grunt work, but the exciting part of this was that he was able to brew his own beers and begin to develop his own recipes on a larger scale.

After his time at White Birch, David found that it was important to continue to sharpen his skills in the world of brewing. This took him to Hill Farmstead in Vermont to begin shadowing and training under Shaun Hill and Dan Suarez. He worked for Shaun in exchange for malts and hops. This was David's idea in order to ensure his ingredient supply for his test batches wouldn't run dry. While he worked under them, he developed his culinary mindset and learned that he needed to leave his mark on every beer he brewed. "I needed to develop a distinct flavor profile and extract every bit of taste out of each brew," said David. "I tend to talk more with chefs than brewers these days because of their understanding of the flavor profiles I am looking to outline." From these conversations, he is able to target two or three flavors and get the most out of them to then translate them into his brews.

It was at this time in his brewing career that David was looking to go out on his own. After toying with the idea for a while, he was pointed in the direction of Blue Lobster Brewing in Hampton, New Hampshire. David pointed out that he likes to brew beers that he likes to drink and hopes others will enjoy them as well. He enjoys dabbling in session-like beers, but every once in a while, he will bring a higher ABV to the market for everyone to enjoy. David's beers at Blue Lobster brought him some high praise in the beer geek world. Ten of his beers are rated ninety and above on RateBeer.com. In the 2013 RateBeer Best Awards, David took a bronze for Wheat (Stalkholm Syndrome) and a bronze for Porter (Ragged Neck Rye) in the category "Best Beers by Style." He also took silver in the same category for Belgian Session and gold for having one of the fifty "World's Top New Beer Releases," his collaboration with Prairie Artisan Ales, Little Lobster on the Prairie.

David has set out on his own since we sat down with him. With the idea of getting his own place off the ground in the coming future, he is optimistic that his brand of brewing and beer style will continue to be revered in the craft brewing world, and we are positive that they will be.

Throughout our travels in putting this book together, we had the opportunity to sit down with countless members of the brewing community in New Hampshire. All had nothing but amazing things to say about David Sakaolsky and his brewing. As mentioned before in this write up, he is a rock star who is just getting started. Cheers to everything he does and will continue to do for the world of craft brewing.

## Appendix I
# Additional Resources

The journey to great craft beer does not end here. As noted before, the craft beer scene is growing rapidly—not just in New Hampshire but also in the entire country. Here is a list of resources that provide the most up-to-date information on the area's craft beer.

## Granite State Brewers Association

*granitestatebrewersassociation.org*

A very important aspect in being part of the brewing community is politics. It costs money to own and operate a brewery, and in New Hampshire, there are many rules and regulations around beer and brewing. The Granite State Brewers Association is an industry organization that seeks to protect and promote the interests of its member breweries on both the promotional and legislative fronts. Interest in craft beer has never been higher, and New Hampshire, like virtually every other state in the United States, is experiencing an explosion in new breweries opening while longtime favorites are beginning exciting new chapters in their businesses' histories. It is important to build a stronger community among brewers and interact with outside people and organizations that are interested in working with brewers. For a number of years, discussions and legislation has come to the floor in Concord that

Granite State Brewers Association logo. *Photo courtesy of Granite State Brewers.*

directly affected brewing as an industry. Now breweries can get involved by being a part of the process.

Another aspect of the GSBA is working with the Department of Travel and Tourism to promote the breweries. All across New Hampshire you can find a brochure with participating breweries and a map so you can plan your own beer adventure.

# BrewNH

## www.nhbeer.org

BrewNH is a 501(c)(6) nonprofit cooperative marketing partnership between New Hampshire's beer distributors and New Hampshire's brewers with one goal: to increase New Hampshire's status as a beer state. This core partnership will serve as a foundation to promote the Granite State's breweries, beer bars, beer stores and other allied businesses through inexpensive initiatives, like social media and web presence. Its website will serve as a holy grail of New Hampshire beer information, including interactive maps, blogs, calendars and other resources. When you have friends and family traveling to New Hampshire, BrewNH will serve as an excellent resource to help anyone find great beer.

## Granite State Growler Tours

### www.nhbeerbus.com

The coolest way to see a handful of breweries on the seacoast is to have someone else drive you. That's what David Adams set out to do when he created the Granite State Growler Tours. His bus, named Greta the Growler Getta, takes craft beer fans on a journey to some of the seacoast's breweries, allowing you to visit multiple breweries in one day without having to drive yourself. Pretzels made from spent grain from local breweries are a much

Granite State Growler Tours logo. *Photo courtesy of David Adams.*

welcomed source of nourishment as you taste your way through the craft beer capital of New Hampshire. There are also coolers on board if you purchase beer on the trip. Keep an eye out for Greta's trips to other areas of New Hampshire as well.

# THE SEACOAST BEVERAGE LAB PODCAST

*www.sblpodcast.com*

The Seacoast Beverage Lab Podcast began in August 2012 as a way to provide beer news in an audio-visual format. The team of five craft beer enthusiasts meets each week and talks about the latest in craft beer news from around the world. The show is also focused on having special guest brewers in to talk about their breweries. Many of the breweries in this book have appeared on the Seacoast Beverage Lab Podcast, including Henniker Brewing Company, Prodigal Brewery, Throwback Brewery, Earth Eagle Brewings, White Birch Brewing, Great Rhythm Brewing Company, Smuttynose Brewing Company and Blue Lobster Brewing Company.

# CARLA COMPANION

*www.thebeerbabe.com*

Carla Companion is a craft beer lover and investigator of all things beer. She started a craft beer website and blog, thebeerbabe.com, in 2007, sharing her thoughts as she explored what was new in beer, as well as brewery visits, trips and "beer adventures." She first found her love of beer after graduating from the University of New Hampshire when she moved to Dover, New Hampshire. While attending graduate school at Antioch University of New England in Keene, she found Twitter and hasn't stopped tweeting about New Hampshire and New England beer since. Moving to Portland in 2009, she found herself surrounded by the Maine beer community, which she is eager to explore. Carla is currently blogging about beer for *Maine Today*.

# Sean Jansen

## *www.2beerguys.com*

Co-founder of 2Beerguys.com, a group of craft beer enthusiasts, and the Craft Beer Guru for the New Hampshire Craft Alliance, Sean's goal is to inspire and grow the craft beer industry, one beer at a time. Although Sean's hometown is in the North Shore of Massachusetts, you will most certainly see him out and about New Hampshire promoting craft beer. Sean also started Portsmouth Beer Week as a way to highlight the craft beer scene on the seacoast.

# Norman Miller

## *blogs.wickedlocal.com/beernut*

Norman Miller has been writing the Beer Nut column for the *MetroWest Daily News* in Framingham, Massachusetts, and *GateHouse Media* since 2006 and the Beer Nut blog for Wickedlocal.com since 2007. He is the author of *Beer Lover's New England* and *Boston Beer: A History of Brewing in the Hub*. He lives in Leominster, Massachusetts, with his dog, two cats and a fully stocked beer fridge named Beatrice.

# NEW HAMPSHIRE BEER BARS AND STORES

O nce you have visited breweries that make the beer, you should venture to a bar to have beer with the locals. These are some of the best places to enjoy New Hampshire beer.

## STRANGE BREW TAVERN

*88 Market Street, Manchester*
*(603) 666-4292 | www.strangebrewtavern.net*

Boasting over one hundred unique taps and a ninety-three rating on Beer Advocate, Strange Brew Tavern is the premier craft beer bar if you are visiting central New Hampshire. It sits quietly tucked away behind city hall but offers bold choices between both its tap list and extensive food menu, which includes recommended beer pairings for its signature dishes. Bring friends and attempt to finish a heaping plate of nachos, or spoil yourself with the Guinness meatballs, complete with mashed potatoes and Guinness gravy. Strange Brew has live music almost every night and outdoor seating when the weather permits. Strange Brew celebrates its fifteenth year in 2014, so stop by and grab a pint to congratulate the bar.

# McGrath's Tavern

*3465 White Mountain Highway, North Conway*
*(603) 733-5955 | www.mcgrathstavernnh.com*

Wanting to drink a Tuckerman or Moat Mountain beer with locals? We asked around and were pointed to McGrath's Tavern. Just across the street from Moat Mountain, this local pub has good food and a draft list worthy of throwing a couple back after a day in the mountains. At night, the tavern has live bands playing, and in nice weather, you can sit outside.

# New England's Tap House Grille

*1292 Hooksett Road, Hooksett*
*(603) 782-5137 | www.taphousenh.com*

With forty-eight beers on tap, New England's Tap House Grille is a craft beer drinker's destination. The tap house features a diverse lineup of local, regional and national brands. At the center of it all are ten rotating taps that showcase local favorites like White Birch Brewing's Ol' Cattywhompus barley wine (the brewery is just across the street), Stone Brewing's Enjoy By and Founder's Bourbon County Stout.

The food is all made from scratch, right down to the burger buns. The menu features several items cooked in a wood-fire oven. Beer-friendly items include the Popper Burger, which has all the makings of a jalapeño popper on top of a burger. Also don't forget to order a side of poutine (seasoned French fries tossed in parmesan cheese and fresh rosemary with peppercorn sherry demi glaze and cheese curd with white truffle oil)!

The atmosphere is contemporary yet comfortable with a friendly staff. Several members have attended training sessions at White Birch Brewing to learn more about the brewing process and different beer styles. The tap house often has brewery promos on Thursday nights and beer dinners throughout the year.

# Press Room

*77 Daniel St, Portsmouth*
*(603) 431-5186 | www.pressroomnh.com*

Opened in 1976, Press Room is an institution in downtown Portsmouth. This is where the locals go to have great beer and watch live music seven days a week. The Press Room features a great tap list of local and hard-to-find craft beer. Breweries love having their beers on tap at the Press Room. This is a great location to find rare beers from local breweries. A major concern for any brewery is how his or her beer will be handled once it leaves the brewery's facility. One bad impression from a beer not treated well by a bar can cost a brewery a lot of customers. Tristan Law, owner of the Press Room, treats beer like a hobbyist handles his or her model airplanes or trains. Go here and tell them we sent you. You will find many of the beers from breweries in this book, and you will have a great time.

# Coat of Arms Pub

*174 Fleet Street, Portsmouth*
*(603) 431-0407 | www.coatofarmspub.com*

You know those places that smell like home? The Coat of Arms British Pub is home for many local beer drinkers and has been serving great food and beer since 1994. What makes the Coat stand out above many other bars is the cask. Cask-conditioned beer, also known as real ale, is beer served without the use of carbon dioxide and can be seen all over the United Kingdom. The Coat of Arms offers three rotating casks from breweries in New England. For the first-time casked beer drinker, you will notice the lack of carbonation, as well as a higher temperature in the beer. What a cask offers is the ability for the brewers to try a lot of crazy ingredients in a beer without making a whole batch. From a Moat Mountain Bone Shaker Brown with rum-soaked oak chips to a Throwback Blonde Ale with raspberries, you will get so much flavor from a casked beer that the last thing on your mind

Brian Aldrich's hand with a pint at the Coat of Arms Pub in Portsmouth, New Hampshire. *Photo courtesy of Michael Meredith.*

will be carbonation. The Coat is also the place to be for rugby and soccer events. The perfect night at the Coat of Arms involves a curry chicken pita, a beer and some snooker, a British sport like pool but with a larger table and different rules.

# WHYM CRAFT BEER CAFE

*3548 Lafayette Road, Portsmouth*
*(603) 501-0478 | www.facebook.com/whymcraftbeer*

This beer bar earns a special place in this book because this is where we started writing this book. WHYM stands for the four main ingredients in beer—Water, Hops, Yeast and Malt. Opened in May 2013, WHYM is the first bar of its kind on the seacoast, being a truly craft beer–focused bar. You will not find mixed drinks unless you blend beers together to

WHYM Craft Beer Café. *Photo courtesy of Michael Meredith.*

see how it tastes. Owners Alex and Gretchen Aviles are New Hampshire natives with a strong passion and extensive knowledge of craft beer.

Alex's inspiration comes from a number of institutions in the craft beer industry. One of his favorite spots is Ebenezer's Pub in Lovell, Maine. His friend Brian Strumke, brew master of Stillwater Artisanal Ales, gave Alex some tips as well as the beer that inspired him, Of Love and Regret, part of Stillwater's Import Series. Alex also had experience overseeing the bar at Cornerstone Artisanal Pizza & Craft Beer in Ogunquit, Maine.

Beer enthusiasts love locating hard-to-find craft beer bar—the more off the beaten path the better. Alex and Gretchen wanted to be off the beaten path, serving the same customers as other great bars/breweries while providing a unique value. It is this mentality that makes WHYM one of the greats. This goes along with the craft beer scene across the globe: less competition and more camaraderie among brewers/bars.

WHYM substitutes a cassette player for TVs, and enjoys cassette Thursdays, for which customers can bring in their own tapes to play. "If you want sports, you will go to a sports bar. If you want Chinese food, you will go to a Chinese restaurant," Alex said. The location of WHYM is actually to its own advantage, located on Route 1 on the middle of what we like to call the Seacoast Beer Trail. You will find beers on tap from the small breweries that only have limited hours like Throwback and Blue Lobster. Most of the time, you will find beers being poured at WHYM only because the brewers know that their beer is going to a bar that appreciates the craft. The draft list is split up into local breweries and a selection of U.S. beers, all hand picked. This is the kind of bar that will make a beer geek freak out, while making someone new to beer feel comfortable. The knowledgeable staff of beertenders will walk you through the beers they have. Alex would like the ability to support every small brewery in New Hampshire. While this is a book about beer, you must know about the food. WHYM offers a variety of local cheeses and meats served alongside spent-grain crackers, as well as full dishes like stout mac and cheese and one of the best burgers you will find on the seacoast, among other tasty treats. Tell Alex and Gretchen we sent you and congratulate yourself on finding one of New Hampshire's greatest beer bars.

# BEER STORES

Taking this book with you on a beer adventure? Here is a list of beer stores located around the breweries in this book that stock their shelves with great beer.

## *Barb's Beer Emporium*

249 Sheep Davis Road, Concord | (603) 369-4501
www.barbsbeeremporium.com

## *Bert's Better Beers*

1100 Hooksett Road, Hooksett | (603) 413-5992
www.bertsbetterbeers.com

## *The Beverage King*

9 Interchange Drive West Lebanon | (603) 298-5817
www.thebeverageking.com

## *Brewtopia*

40 Washington Street, Keene | (603) 357-7773
www.brewtopianh.com

## *Craft Beer Cellar*

767 Islington Street #1D, Portsmouth | (603) 373-0993
www.craftbeercellar.com/portsmouth

## *The Drinkery*

2 Young Road, Londonderry | (603) 434-1012
www.thedrinkeryshop.com

## *Littleton Food Co-op*

43 Bethlehem Road, Littleton | (603) 444-2800
www.littletoncoop.org

## *Top Shelf Brews*

826 Lafayette Road, Hampton | (603) 601-2894
www.topshelfbrewsstore.com

## *The Vista Country Store*

10 Hurricane Mountain Road, North Conway | (603) 356-5084

# BIBLIOGRAPHY

Aldrich, Brian. "Kate the Great Day 2012 Live Blog." Available at http://www.seacoastbeveragelab.com/2012/03/04/kate-great-day-2012-live-blog. March 2012.

"Aloha Belgian Style Pale." Available at http://www.whitebirchbrewing.com/home/apprentice-program/aloha. August 2010.

"Broustaris." Available at http://www.whitebirchbrewing.com/home/apprentice-program/aloha. August 2012.

"Financial Report 2013." Anheuser-Busch InBev.

"Frank Jones." Available at http://www.rustycans.com/HISTORY/jones.html. 2001.

Garnick, Darren. "Jason Sanderson: The Most Interesting (Wolfman) in New Hampshire." Available at http://www.nhmagazine.com/December-2013/Jason-Sanderson-The-Most-Interesting-Wolfman-in-New-Hampshire. December 2013.

"HB1172." Available at http://www.nhliberty.org/bills/view/2012/HB1172. June 2012.

Kaplan, Scott. "Legal Eagle." Available at http://ybnonline.brewingnews.com/publication/?i=178180&p=28. October/November 2013.

Knoblock, Glenn A., and James T. Gunter. *Brewing in New Hampshire.* Mount Pleasant, SC: Arcadia Publishing, 2004.

"178:12—A Nano Brewery License." Available at http://www.gencourt.state.nh.us/rsa/html/XIII/178/178-12-a.htm. September 2013.

"Rate Beer Best Awards." Available at http://www.ratebeer.com/RateBeerBest. 2014.

# BIBLIOGRAPHY

Shea, Chris. "On Beer and Brewing: So You Want to Be a Brewer, Eh?" Available at http://www.nhmagazine.com/December-2013/Jason-Sanderson-The-Most-Interesting-Wolfman-in-New-Hampshire. December 2013.

"6,324 Pints of Beer on the Wall." Available at http://www.kickstarter.com/projects/1122986730/6324-pints-on-the-wall. May 2012.

"2014 New Hampshire Brewery Map." Available at http://www.visitnh.gov/uploads/itineraries/2014/NH-Brewery-Map-2014.pdf. 2014.

"Valley Malt." Available at http://valleymalt.com/find-our-malt. 2010.

# INDEX

Great Rhythm Brewing Company 7,
    95, 96, 112
Greg Ouellette 30
gruit 85, 86

## H

Hampton 37, 39, 100, 107
Hassan, Maggie 54
hefeweizen 56, 82, 103
Heilshorn, Butch 85
Herlicka, Bill 75, 78, 106
Hewes, Geoff 89
Hewes, Tamsin 89
Hill Farmstead 106
Hobbs Farm 83
Hooksett 75, 106, 120

## I

IncrediBREW 30, 102
IPA 24, 26, 35, 42, 47, 48, 56, 62, 78,
    82, 83, 90, 93, 102, 105

## J

Johnson, Stephen 70
Jones, Tyler 24, 26, 27, 96

## K

Keene 43, 45, 46, 112, 121
kolsch 43, 77, 100
Kona Brewing Company 56, 57

## L

lager 21, 47
Lee, Annette 81, 84
Lee, Bill 72, 74
Leonard, Dan 89
Lincoln 51, 69
Littleton 61, 103, 121
Littleton Food Co-op 121
Londonderry 89, 121
Lubold, Tony 47, 48

## M

Manchester 33, 35, 43, 101, 105
Marley, Rik 60, 61, 62, 64, 103
Martha's Exchange Restaurant &
    Brewery 26, 29, 30, 31, 33, 46
McDonald, Alex 85, 86, 87
McDonald, Gretchen 85, 87
McGrath's Tavern 116
Merrimack 17, 19, 20
Milly's Tavern 33, 35, 36
Moat Mountain Smokehouse &
    Brewery 7, 69, 70, 71, 72, 74,
    75, 116, 117
Moore, Matt 72
Mott, Todd 10, 11, 23, 24, 26, 47
Mullett, Ben 43, 45

## N

Nashua 29, 30, 31, 33, 102
Neve, Kirsten 65
New England's Tap House Grille 116
New London 59
Noonan, Greg 41, 47, 48
Northampton (MA) 21, 22, 23, 25
North Conway 43, 69, 70
North Hampton 81
North Woodstock 49, 51, 52, 54

## O

One Love Brewery 99, 100
Oulette, Greg 26

## P

pale ale 23, 24, 31, 39, 42, 62, 65, 66,
    72, 75, 86, 90, 95, 96, 100, 103
Paquette, Dan 91
pilsener 72, 82
porter 33, 40, 42, 82, 83, 86, 91, 93,
    103, 107
Portsmouth 7, 9, 10, 11, 21, 22, 23, 24,
    25, 26, 27, 30, 33, 37, 38, 39,
    43, 47, 48, 55, 56, 75, 80, 83,

# ABOUT THE AUTHORS

## BRIAN ALDRICH

Brian Aldrich started writing about beer for his blog Seacoast Beverage Lab in March 2010. Along with his blog and craft beer podcast, Brian is the beer master at the Sheraton Portsmouth Harborside Hotel, providing guests with a unique craft beer experience. He lives in Newfields, New Hampshire, with his wife, Lisa, and dog Madison. Visit him at www.seacoastbeveragelab.com.

## MICHAEL MEREDITH

Michael started his love for craft beer in 2011 after graduating from Endicott College with his masters in business administration. Co-host of the Seacoast Beverage Lab Podcast since 2012, Michael enjoys exploring all the craft beer world has to offer. Michael works in the beer, wine and spirits industry for a promotional products firm and lives in Salem, Massachusetts.